T0215034

AGILE PRODUCT DEVELOPMENT

HOW TO DESIGN INNOVATIVE PRODUCTS THAT CREATE CUSTOMER VALUE

Tathagat Varma

Apress®

ISBN-13 (pbk): 978-1-4842-1068-0

ISBN-13 (electronic): 978-1-4842-1067-3

Managing Director: Welmoed Spahr
Acquisitions Editor: Celestin Suresh John
Developmental Editor: Douglas Pundick
Editorial Board: Steve Anglin, Mark Beckner, Gary Cornell, Louise Corrigan, James DeWolf, Jonathan Gennick, Robert Hutchinson, Celestin Suresh John, Michelle Lowman, James Markham, Susan McDermott, Matthew Moodie, Jeffrey Pepper, Douglas Pundick, Ben Renow-Clarke, Gwenan Spearing, Matt Wade
Coordinating Editor: Rita Fernando
Copy Editor: Ann Dickson
Compositor: SPi Global
Indexer: SPi Global

Distributed to the book trade worldwide by Springer Science+Business Media New York, 233 Spring Street, 6th Floor, New York, NY 10013. Phone 1-800-SPRINGER, fax (201) 348-4505, e-mail orders-ny@springer-sbm.com, or visit www.springer.com. Apress Media, LLC is a California LLC and the sole member (owner) is Springer Science + Business Media Finance Inc (SSBM Finance Inc). SSBM Finance Inc is a Delaware corporation.

For information on translations, please e-mail rights@apress.com, or visit www.apress.com.

Apress and friends of ED books may be purchased in bulk for academic, corporate, or promotional use. eBook versions and licenses are also available for most titles. For more information, reference our Special Bulk Sales–eBook Licensing web page at www.apress.com/bulk-sales.

Any source code or other supplementary materials referenced by the author in this text is available to readers at www.apress.com. For detailed information about how to locate your book's source code, go to www.apress.com/source-code/.

Apress Business: The Unbiased Source of Business Information

Apress business books provide essential information and practical advice, each written for practitioners by recognized experts. Busy managers and professionals in all areas of the business world—and at all levels of technical sophistication—look to our books for the actionable ideas and tools they need to solve problems, update and enhance their professional skills, make their work lives easier, and capitalize on opportunity.

Whatever the topic on the business spectrum—entrepreneurship, finance, sales, marketing, management, regulation, information technology, among others—Apress has been praised for providing the objective information and unbiased advice you need to excel in your daily work life. Our authors have no axes to grind; they understand they have one job only—to deliver up-to-date, accurate information simply, concisely, and with deep insight that addresses the real needs of our readers.

It is increasingly hard to find information—whether in the news media, on the Internet, and now all too often in books—that is even-handed and has your best interests at heart. We therefore hope that you enjoy this book, which has been carefully crafted to meet our standards of quality and unbiased coverage.

We are always interested in your feedback or ideas for new titles. Perhaps you'd even like to write a book yourself. Whatever the case, reach out to us at editorial@apress.com and an editor will respond swiftly. Incidentally, at the back of this book, you will find a list of useful related titles. Please visit us at www.apress.com to sign up for newsletters and discounts on future purchases.

The Apress Business Team

To the ever-changing
software industry
for making me
a lifelong learner

Contents

About the Author

Tathagat Varma has been involved with high-tech software product development since 1991 when he began working with Defense Research and Development Organisation (DRDO). He has subsequently worked with Siemens Telecom, Philips Medical Systems and Philips Digital Networks divisions, Huawei Technologies, McAfee, NetScout Systems, Yahoo!, and [24]7 Innovation Labs in significant technical and leadership roles. His key roles include being a member of the senior management team at Huawei, starting up and heading India operations for NetScout Systems (when it was known as Sniffer Technologies prior to acquisition), and heading the business operations at Yahoo! R&D India. In 2014, he founded Thought Leadership, a knowledge creation firm that adopts an interdisciplinary approach to solving organizational problems and offers high-end consulting and coaching on strategy, agility, innovation, and leadership to product development organizations.

Tathagat holds an MS in computer science from JK Institute of Applied Physics and Technology, Allahabad University, India, a post-graduate certificate in HR management from Xavier Labor Research Institute School of Business and Human Resources (XLRI), Jamshedpur, India, and certificates in business leadership skills, executive leadership, and financial management from Cornell University, USA. In addition, he is also certified PMP, PRINCE2 Registered Practitioner, CSP, CSM, CSPO, Scaled Agile Framework Program Consultant (SAFe SPC), Management 3.0 Practitioner, and Senior Member of IEEE and ACM.

Tathagat has volunteered with PMI Innovation and New Product Development Community of Practice, IEEE Technology Management Council, Agile India, Agile Leadership Network, and several other voluntary organizations. He has been a mentor at startup accelerators such as Google Launchpad, First100Sales, NASSCOM 10,000 Startups, Sandbox Startups, and NUMA, and has been a visiting faculty teaching project management, business ethics, design thinking, lean startup, and agile software development courses. He has authored and presented over 150+ papers and talks at national and international conferences and other corporate sessions. He blogs at www.managewell.net, and his slide decks are hosted at http://slideshare .net/managewell.

Tathagat also holds the unique distinction of being the youngest member of the 13th Indian Scientific Expedition to Antarctica, where he participated as a computer scientist and stayed at the Indian permanent station Maitri for a period of 16 icy months in 1993–1995. He studied data communication between India and Antarctica and the effects of unique weather conditions on life-support systems in Antarctica. He thinks everyone should at least spend a summer in Antarctica!

About the Technical Reviewer

Swapnil Saurav is a Project Manager with JDA Software, Hyderabad (India). He has earned the reputation as a perceptive and practical troubleshooter with the unique ability to solve large-scale problems often deemed too challenging for others. With more than 12 years of work experience handling and managing large and complex software projects, Swapnil has a passion for the supply chain with a focus on retail and manufacturing industries and an uncompromising commitment to quality and outstanding customer service. An ambitious, creative, and highly motivated individual, Swapnil has been invited as keynote speaker at various industry forums, and he has a passion for teaching and developing leaders for tomorrow. He holds a BS in computer science engineering (Visweswaraih Technological University), an MS (BITS Pilani), and an MBA (S.P. Jain Institute of Management and Research). His motto is to "learn everyday" and is currently pursuing a PhD in management from the University of Petroleum and Energy Studies. His personal website is www.swapnil.asia.

Acknowledgments

No one can truly appreciate what it takes to write a book until one begins to actually start writing it! Having been blogging for over ten years, I was under the naive impression that my transition from an amateur blogger to a book author would be a linear one. If anything, the last year has been a great learning experience—and a humbling one, too!

First and foremost, I must thank the awesome team at Apress for offering me such a wonderful opportunity to write this book. When Celestin "discovered" me through my blog post on LinkedIn and asked me if I would like to write a book, it sounded straight out of a movie plot. Over the next several months, he painstakingly guided me through the entire process of preparing an initial proposal for the book, and helped me finalize it. Subsequently, when the real action started in terms of writing down the chapters, Rita was always there. She was the scrum master who was always there to help. She gave me that gentle nudge to make sure that even as I was running behind schedule, I did everything that needed to be done to catch up and deliver the chapter in potentially shippable increments. Thanks, Celestin and Rita, for not giving up on me!

I know that a large team from Apress was there in the background working on this book, and I want to call out Matt Moodie, Ann Dickson and SPi Global for all their efforts. In addition, the review feedback and critical inputs by reviewers is an author's lifeline—that is the first feedback on a product that is still quite raw. I want to offer my sincere thanks to Swapnil Saurav for his technical review.

I can't thank my professional network enough for enriching my learning journey through the years—my former employers, my clients, managers, colleagues, team members, students, readers of my blog, audience to my talks, and the noblest of them all—the fellow volunteers. Thanks for all the support and learning opportunities, and for making me a better professional every single day.

My wife, Shikha, and son, Chanakya, deserve an extra special round of applause. The year 2015 was an especially tough year for us as I was busy building my newly started venture, Chanakya was busy writing his senior secondary school exams and Shikha was busy helping him prepare for his college admissions. Despite all that chaos, I managed to get this book out only because of their encouragement and understanding. Thanks for putting up with all the discomfort, but you guys were awesome, and your support was so good, I can't wait to get started on my next book!

Finally, despite all the diligent efforts of the editorial team and reviewers, I must accept responsibility for all the mistakes and shortcomings in this book. Let me know how I can make this book better.

Introduction

In the past man has been first. In the future the System will be first.

—Frederick Winslow Taylor, *The Principles of Scientific Management*, 1911

With all due regards to Taylor, this one single line from the world of manufacturing has perhaps caused more damage to the entire knowledge industry in the last hundred years than everything else put together. During the twentieth century, we blindly adopted this mantra without realizing that manufacturing and knowledge creation are two different worlds—they are like chalk and cheese in that what works in one doesn't necessarily work in the other. Manufacturing is fundamentally a production problem, and knowledge creation is more like a design problem. Most certainly, there can't be a "system" to developing new and innovative products—we must leverage human creativity, judgment and continuous learning to solve the problems effectively.

While the production world was all about predictability, control, "Plan A," organization, accuracy, structure, tools, automation, and so on, the world of knowledge was full of messy creation, cognitive work, experimentation, mistakes, adaptation, "Plan B," iteration, prototyping, serendipity, wicked problems, people dependency, and so on. The methods that worked well for production (such as the waterfall model, frameworks like PMBoK and CMMi, and standards like ISO9000) were well suited for a world where a problem was all about producing a replica of something that had been already designed—for example, assembling cars or manufacturing mobile phones. However, these methods, standards, and frameworks were fairly useless when it came to "managing" a creative process for they sought false value in accuracy, predictability, repeatability, and efficiency when these were not even the key drivers of value in a constantly changing world. Having been part of several endeavors where we tried to tame the software process using industrial-era thinking, I realized the naivety and futility of our efforts. Over time, I had opportunities to learn better ways to build products, and this book is my attempt to put it all together.

In this book, I have tried to establish the journey of an idea as it is born, and as it fights for survival and grows on the back of market and end-user validation—starting with high-level feedback on something that might simply be a doodle on a cocktail napkin to fleshed-out working software that allows users to interact with it. Conventional methods assume we are solving the right problem and we know enough about the right solution. Unfortunately, this set of deadly assumptions leads to over 90% mortality of new product initiatives and startups. In today's world, this could be fatal not just from the cost point of view, but also even more importantly from the loss of the window of opportunity.

Irrespective of your field, the ideas shared in this book could help you align your level of investment into the solutioning commensurate with the level of problem validation. If you have chosen a wrong idea, a wrong market, or prematurely chosen a wrong solution, this book will help you fail faster and fail cheaper so that you don't waste an inordinate amount of time, effort, and money in chasing the wrong problem. Of course, if you are on the right track, this book will teach you how to establish checkpoints along the way to systematically mitigate the risks in new product development using agile thinking.

Preamble

Back to Agility

... And, unfortunately, I think the time has proven me right. The word "agile" has been subverted to the point where it is effectively meaningless, and what passes for an agile community seems to be largely an arena for consultants and vendors to hawk services and products.

So I think it is time to retire the word "Agile."

...We've lost the word agile. Let's try to hang on to agility. Let's keep it meaningful, and let's protect it from those who would take the soul of our ideas in order to sell it back to us.

—**Dave Thomas,** Agile Manifesto Signatory, Keynote address[1]
at Agile India 2014, Bangalore

Dave was not just ranting when he delivered his keynote talk, which was actually his first one since co-authoring the Agile Manifesto in 2001. Sitting in rapt attention in the audience, many of us could relate to what's been happening. While in 2001, the original signatories of the Agile Manifesto created a powerful and aspirational vision for software development and established its first principles, the current reality seemed to be very distant from what was originally propounded.

---

[1]Agile is Dead (Long Live Agility), http://pragdave.me/blog/2014/03/04/time-to-kill-agile/.

Having been given consultant-ese and vendor-driven commandments of implementing and achieving agility through specialized, costly, and proprietary tools, we are in perpetual danger of being run over by slick marketing brochures that promise to teach everything except, perhaps, agility. A practitioner-led movement that started out with the goal of restoring agility to individuals and teams so they could shape their own destiny had gradually deteriorated to a one-size-fit-all template at the mercies of consultants and toolmakers. The notion of agility has been reduced to following an "agile process" out of the box—whatever that means!

The moment we say we follow a certain "agile process," we are essentially saying that there is this one great process that we have chosen to follow that works for all seasons and all reasons, and, by the way, it is an "agile process" so we can now claim to be agile. Following an agile process makes us agile. Yay!

Sadly, this is a farce.

The reality is that following an agile process, or any process for that matter, makes us "un-agile."

Agility is all about nurturing a mindset that enables us to constantly adapt to a rapidly evolving situation and look for more effective ways to solve a problem. To that end, an "agile process" is an oxymoron because the moment we call a given sequence of steps a "process," we basically nail down all its moving parts in order to construct some kind of a repeatable finite state machine— something where there is a finite and fixed number of states with clear rules that govern transition among them—with the "assurance" that following this process will lead to agility. Needless to say, such thinking kills any element of "agility" right then and there!

Imagine driving with your family for a vacation to a new place out of town. If you have a route map, you are likely to have comfort in knowing what to expect in terms of distance to the destination, highways to take, establishments to stop for food and gas, and so on. You are likely to follow the map verbatim lest you be stranded in the middle of nowhere on a cold, rainy night with a hungry, tired, and upset family. If your map matches the terrain, it essentially means you are replaying a script that hundreds or thousands of people have already played before you. All you need to do is simply follow the instructions and you will get to your destination. There is no inherent reason for not reaching the destination, other than perhaps inclement weather conditions, unexpected car trouble, or a passenger with motion sickness. However, imagine that one of the towns you are passing through is holding a carnival and your family wants to spend a day there before proceeding farther. If you have watertight plans that don't allow for accommodating such last-minute or even in-process "changes," you risk losing the benefits from those changes (in this case, a great family time) by simply sticking to a fixed plan.

Let's further say that your map is a few years old (and which map isn't?), so chances are that the terrain might not match the map—some old roads have been closed, some new ones have opened, a few new pit stops have come to your attention, and there are some temporary traffic diversions. Most of them won't be reflected on your map. Are you still going to follow the map?[2] Perhaps some of us would rather follow the map as it is written than adapt to the current conditions. We might get confused, delayed, or even stuck in a zombie town, a consequence of what happens when we continue to stick to the standard process even when the ground conditions have changed. We have a Plan A that has been meticulously planned over months, and the success of the project lies in its flawless execution, even if blindly following the plan could lead us to more problems than it was meant to solve. I call such mindless compliance as "operation successful, but the patient died."

However, if you are like most people, you will not likely trust the map beyond a point. The map will only serve as a guide at a macro level, but you will have to rely on other better means to find your way at a micro level. In India, it is very common for travelers to simply pull the car over to the side of the road (and sometimes even on the road itself!) and ask any of the local people for directions. And since you don't know if you got the right answer from one, you ask another, and another…! But what if it raining or it is late night and you can't find anyone on the road to ask?

Luckily, we have GPS. If our GPS is up-to-date, it will tell us which roads have changed (say, from a two-way street into a one-way street) or new gas stations that have opened. As a result, you will be able to use GPS to plan and replan your destination. Taken an exit one too soon? Or, missed the U-turn? No problem. The GPS will recalculate so you can get to a new route that eventually takes you to your destination. As opposed to the previous two examples, we are not sticking to a Plan A nor are we assuming that the ground condition will remain static. As the situation changes, we change our priorities and replan the rest of the journey—going from Plan A to a Plan B, Plan C, or even a Plan D. We are constantly accommodating factors that are beyond our control. Instead of either ignoring them until they become inevitable, we are responding to them in time so that we can stay focused on the end objective.

Is there a predictable process to what we are doing? Not really. One could argue that the "atomic constituents" of what it takes to reach our destination are still the same—filling up the gas tank, changing the flat tire, driving, taking breaks, and so on are the same whether you have a map or use a GPS for directions. However, the way we schedule these constituents or interweave them in a given sequence, as in the last case, is not always known a priori. Or, even if it is planned a priori, we recognize that adapting to immediate changes

---

[2]There is a saying in the Swiss Army manual—when the map and the terrain disagree, trust the terrain!

is more valuable than simply sticking to a predetermined routine (that was created sitting at the dining table away from the ground zero, and hence a plan that could be very romantic and very different from the reality on the road!). We might have a big grain size plan (for example drive 150 miles, stop for refreshments, go to a water park, and then resume driving at 4 p.m.) and, in many cases, we might also do some research on the available options, but as we get closer to the point of action or a point of decision, we might change our plan without ever worrying about how are we going to complete the rest of the journey. In some cases, we might decide to go completely "off script" because we see something that was not on the original to-do list, but seems to be too good to pass.

Luckily, software development is not very different in terms of its meta-approach to building systems (though one could argue that the "atomic operations" are fundamentally more complex than, say, driving to another town, and the judgment on what to do next only comes with deep experience). When you have done a given task dozens of times before, you need to find a way to "standardize" the "process" so that it can be accomplished by anyone without too much thinking (in other words, reduce the wait times or decisions by making it known in advance) and without making too many mistakes. However, when you take the road less traveled, you don't have enough data points to help you "standardize" the "process." While you still have to rely on fundamental atomic operations of problem-solving, you can't quite say, with enough certainty, as to what specific process you would follow to solve the problem. And, by corollary, you can't say by when will you be finished. The general approach you might take is to formulate a hypothesis and then test it as soon as possible without expending too much of time, effort, or money. The 1938 Nobel Prizewinner in Physics, Enrico Fermi, said it so well: "There are two possible outcomes: if the result confirms the hypothesis, then you've made a measurement. If the result is contrary to the hypothesis, then you've made a discovery."

Would you call this approach to problem-solving a "process"? Or, does it sound more like a very haphazard and chaotic way to solve problems—something that can't be "measured" or "monitored," and, hence, can't be "controlled"? Well, depending on what problem we are trying to solve, we might need to decide what solution to use. If the problem hasn't been solved before and looks more like an "unknown-unknown" problem, there is no way you are going to have divine insight that leads you straight into the solution without making dozens of mistakes during the journey. However, if you want to solve a "known-known" problem that has been already solved hundreds of time before, you recognize that all systemic uncertainties and complexities have been ironed out by people before you, so all you need to focus is on carefully executing it.

A process, by definition, has connotations of being a series of fixed steps that, when repeated in the pre-defined sequence, will lead to the desired and already known outcome.

However, can we solve all kinds of problems using a process?

Spectrum of Problems

Clearly, the world seems to be full of problems that we have solved before as well as problems that we are yet to solve. Sometimes we call the second category "unknown-unknown" problems, whereas the ones that we have solved before are called "known-known."

In this context, I like the Stacey Matrix (Figure 1-1) that helps us build a good thinking model on how to segregate problems into big buckets or category of problem types.

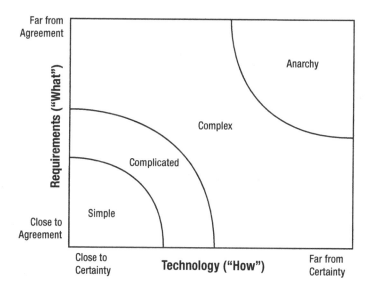

Figure 1-1. Each problem is unique and different

Solving Simple Problems

When we know enough about the problem to be solved and the technology we are going to use to solve it, it typically falls into the simple quadrant, or the "known-known" part of the problem spectrum. Say, for example, we want to produce 10,000 writing pens. Would you call the problem fundamentally a "known-known" problem, never mind the fact that it might require some complex machining technology? What would be the best process to solve such a problem? Given that the problem has been solved before and all that is needed is to execute the specific steps in a fixed sequence, it is more like an execution problem and could perhaps be best solved using waterfall thinking (linear, sequential, fixed steps that require the product to be built essentially in a single pass). What about the quality? Well, we could apply the principles of statistical process control to measure, monitor, and control product quality. In this class of problems, mistakes are typically a manifestation of poor execution, and by reverse corollary, more management control typically leads to better awareness about them.

What would be the best way to solve such problems? Frameworks such as PMBoK, CMMi, and Six Sigma sound like a great way. The process is largely predictive, so a plan could be built around all knowns. If there are any unknowns during execution, they could be addressed using risk management techniques or by creating appropriate time or resource buffers. The variations in execution could be monitored using statistical process control techniques and brought under a process improvement loop such as a PDCA loop using principles of six sigma.

Solving Complicated and Complex Problems

Let's go to the next point in this continuum. Let's say we know enough about the requirements to solve the problem, but not enough about the technology—or vice versa. What would be a good way to solve such class of problems? Since we don't understand the "cause-and-effect" relationships very well in this case, we will need to conduct experiments to "uncover" them. Since one of the variables is known, it allows us to experiment. Based on the results (which allow us to establish the cause- and-effect relationship more completely since only one variable is unknown), we can adapt our hypotheses for the next set of learning. However, we must recognize that the fundamental nature of problem-solving shifts to learning to quite an extent and, hence, must be open to experimentation and even making mistakes in that process. This is quite a contrast to the simple class of problems, where making mistakes would be akin to poor performance. However, in a complicated or a complex problem, it might be the fastest way for us to accomplish our goals! So, if we start blaming people for mistakes, we might be sending the wrong message, and any chance of solving such problems could be foregone.

By design, agile methods suit this class of problems well. For example, we know how to build an e-commerce web site. However, we don't know what will people like to buy or how would people like a given set of products to be presented (visual, or multimedia, or textual) or what design will suit best the product (material design, minimalistic design, and so on) … the list is endless.

Instead of guessing at these aspects and building a product that people don't like, we could take baby steps and make key hypotheses around the most critical open issues, while learning incrementally. At the same time, we would be establishing the cause-and-effect relationship before moving on to the next stage of problem-solving. Understanding these cause-and-effect relationships among different moving parts is perhaps the most important part of problem-solving in this class of problems, and agile thinking provides some helpful ideas (as we will examine in this book).

Solving Anarchy Problems

What happens when you reach the anarchy or the "unknown-unknown" category of problems? Would you know, a priori, the cause-and-effect relationships at play? Are there logical or analytical tools or methods available that can help us solve the problem? Not very likely. The success depends largely on making intelligent hypotheses and quickly testing them so that we can "discover" them. The key is to prototype the ideas using the smallest amount of time, effort, and money possible and learn before making the next mistake. Again, making mistakes is the most appropriate form of learning in solving such problems and, hence, must be encouraged. Of course, we are not saluting people for making obvious mistakes, but for making new and intelligent mistakes—the ones that help validate a key hypothesis faster than your competitors and save invaluable time (and money).

Can we solve such problems using a "scripted process" such as a waterfall, or even an "inspect-and-adapt" process like the agile? A scripted process is clearly out of question because we can't accurately forecast all the nooks and crannies, humps and potholes that we happen upon on the untraveled road. Agile thinking could help, but it does suffer a limitation in terms of the fundamental reason what are we solving—the fundamental aim is exploration and the basic unit of progress is the number of ideas that have been validated. Agile thinking is more close-ended and has been designed to bring software processes under more empirical control rather than address the so-called "fuzzy front-end of innovation" where the end is often not known when we start the journey. Most successful companies today did not initially have a well-defined product vision or a backlog that they could simply go and run with. They had a big bold idea, often called the founder's vision, or a "leap of faith hypothesis" in Lean Startup parlance, around which they designed series of experiments to validate thoroughly. Often the idea had to be discarded and the founders had to "pivot" to something else that sounded more reasonable and promising. On the other hand, agile thinking is more execution-focused and places emphasis on delivering value to the customer with each iteration. Unfortunately, in this class of problems, we are still very far from discovering the true source of value to the customers.

Solving Problems in Software Development

In the late 1990s, the software process improvement (SPI) movement was at its peak in most parts of the tech world, and most certainly in Bangalore. After all, with some 50% of CMM Level 5 assessed companies being in this single city alone, there was a great momentum across the industry (and often a sense of immense pride in it). I remember recruitment ads and marketing brochure milking those credentials every day. I was also part of two product MNCs that went in for CMM Level 5 assessment, including an ISO 9000 TickIT at one of them. And when I look back, I still can't figure out why we did it. Perhaps, we simply had nothing else to help solve the problems. So, when the new-age process wave came along, we all simply latched on to it. But that still doesn't answer why we did it? IT/ITES outsourcing companies had at least some commercial reasons—after all, they had to tick the RFP checklist (especially for the large corporations and government clients who needed the comfort of safety before deciding to outsource to a third-world country twelve time zones away), but why did product companies do it? I still don't have an answer that I really believe in.

The process improvement movement created reams of Dilbertesque documentation that sought to standardize software development processes, still predominantly waterfall, in a highly prescriptive manner. With the entire focus on predictability of delivery, quality by inspection, and execution to the budget, the desired outcome was to deliver all the features as per the contract within the limits of the allotted time, cost, and quality as mutually agreed upon. The subsequent changes were consigned to change control board (CCB), and were often a way to wrestle more time, effort, and money from the customers. Accommodating any new requirement in a waterfall cycle meant extending the entire delivery timelines, even for the initially envisaged and clearly known upfront requirements, at the expense of the customer. So, agility was not something that we offered as the default with our process, or as a core value to our customers, or even as a strategic competitive advantage over our competitors. Instead, we charged our customers while they waited through the extended delivery timelines!

The entire project planning was a wishful thinking at best and a managerial farce at worst. In one product MNC that shall go unnamed, we were once sitting and "estimating" a large system. There were several folks who had more experience than me, so I was more like looking at their faces and hoping to learn a trick or two on how they pulled that magic. To my dismay, they would pull out numbers like 5-man-years or 12-man-years of effort with such atomic precision that I was completely floored. Especially given that there was no basis for coming up with those numbers—hell, we didn't even know the "size" of what we were signing up for, let alone the capability of people whom we were yet to hire for this project! In just a few hours, we had "estimated" over 100-man-years of project in complex space of telecommunication software for ATM switches. That meeting was an epiphany for me—I was getting close to understanding why software projects were always running late with the engineers spending all their evenings and weekends at work. Thankfully, the project was scrapped after a few months.

When I moved to a more process-driven company, we applied some common sense and a bit more software science. If the total "size" of a project was, say, 10KLOC and engineer's productivity was an average of 20LOC/person-day (averaged through the entire development lifecycle), and the project was needed in five months, then we needed five team members. The challenge was to estimate the size, for which we had to first freeze the scope of project and identify all requirements clearly. Did that work? Not really. In one product that I was once leading, we were working on the complex domain of digital video broadcasting for the first time. We had no clue what to expect. We estimated 3KLOC of software in C/C++ to be written, which ended up being some 30KLOC. Estimating LOC was helpful because it helped determine the ROM size needed for the embedded software. Was there a better way to solve that problem? Not to any of us on the project back then.

When it came to planning the project, it was essentially parametric estimation. Once you knew the size, it was easy to come up with effort and schedule trade-offs if you knew the complexity and productivity numbers. However, with the uncertainty being what it was and the nature of project planning being a fixed end date and fixed budget, one had to introduce a fair amount of buffers to raise confidence levels to 80–90% or more. Despite having buffers, something would invariably derail the project and delay it—sometimes even sending it in a deep tailspin. Since that's how most of the projects were run in those days (just checkout the Standish Group Report stats from the early '90s until 2004), it was not completely unacceptable.

This was also an old world of large customers who would typically ask large vendors to build or maintain large systems. Teams would be given a multi-year budget to deliver a dot release where all requirements were priority one. No one wanted, or had the need, to ever see an early version of the product, and certainly there was no urgency to revisit requirement every few weeks—both the technology and markets remained largely static over reasonably long periods of time. We essentially shipped hope and dreams on the back of status reports, keeping stakeholders happy for the most part. Despite its known shortfalls, waterfall still was the preferred way to solve problems in this old world. If there were stringent constraints on some parameter (mostly it would be around delivery schedule), we would bake in a risk management and contingency buffer during project planning to buy us more people or simply have dollars to ensure that delivery commitment was not seriously impacted.

However, the post-dotcom world changed it all.

In terms of the technology, the focus was increasingly on Internet-based software, even though the tech stack was not fully mature or proven. Due to the market crash, there wasn't enough money or interest to fund large and complex multi-year projects, and the investors, executives, and financial controllers were looking for faster ROI. Not only were the project budgets much smaller immediately after the dotcom meltdown (and later again, more decisively, after the global financial meltdown in 2008), the timelines were also much shorter and the products were more customer-focused than tech-focused as in the past. Internet technologies started evolving and getting obsoleted at a mindboggling pace, which essentially meant that large companies with their archaic planning cycles and bloated execution methods couldn't keep pace with such an "agile" world. The proliferation of consumer devices in small businesses and homes impacted the nature of software consumption and, in turn, the software development. The focus clearly went from being predominantly B2B (or rather LB2LB—large business to large business) to B2C. Like the investors, these customers were equally cost-conscious and were not willing to wait long periods of time only to get a bad product. For the first time in tech history, hundreds and thousands of entrepreneurs sprang up all over the world (several of them H1B visa holders returning home after being on either a Y2K project or a dotcom that went down, or who simply got laid off from a large company). They all had technical chops and a certain level of market understanding, and now, thanks to advancements in communications and collaboration technologies, they could be sitting anywhere in the world and serving global customers.

Clearly, the old methods of using waterfall or V-model were inadequate for this new world. While the Agile Manifesto called out better ways to develop software in 2001, it didn't exactly catch on like wildfire. Lack of enough proof points, especially with conventional enterprises and large projects, was a major issue. As a result, agile methods were perceived only for the small, web-based projects. Specific methodologies such as Scrum, XP, Crystal, and DSDM were available, but without much context into large systems or systems software. Hence, they were typically rejected by the large enterprises (who only needed any flimsy reason to justify and retain the archaic ways to develop software and run businesses).

Agile was the new kid on the block, promising all kinds of new magic tricks, but it was not clear how much of the magic was actually possible. In an industry used to seeing new silver bullets every now and then, and guided by "predictions" such as the famous "No Silver Bullet" by practitioner-luminaries like Fred Brooks, agile was seen as one more "silver bullet." And in a typical old-school mindset, it made sense to stick to the imperfect present than to embrace the uncertain future.

At the developer and even at team level, however, agile methods were slowly making great inroads. Individuals and teams were discovering newer ways to plan and execute projects using small time slices, capture and understand requirements better, manage changes more gracefully even later in the cycle, and create much shorter, earlier, and frequent feedback loops with their customers. Also, this was pure salvation to an engineer's soul. Sadly, not much upper management was buying into this. In several cases, there were other organizational inefficiencies outside the software team at play, so even if the software team made fantastic improvements in performance, most of that vanished when scaled up at the organization level.[3] Justifiably, agile didn't make much financial sense under those scenarios.

In its initial days, agile was also perceived as too much of an anti-establishment. In particular, scrum came up with fancy stuff like the "chicken and pigs" metaphor and the agile community nodded their heads collectively in agreement. Clearly, the message being driven was that management was evil, so let's fix it. Agile methods sought to create an alternate reality in which there was little role for any form of management, let alone having a project manager. Needless to say, such radical methods were seen too communist to be adopted by companies, especially old-school companies looking to solve their problems without being forced to completely change their existing management structures or policies.

No points for guessing what happens when you point fingers at your sponsors?

Over time, businesses were forced to adopt elements of agile, while the agile community was also forced to re-examine its approach. At almost every organization where I worked or consulted, there was a home blend approach, taking some of the "standard" framework and adapting it with the unique constraints of one's business. Some people in the agile community believe such methods are neither agile nor waterfall, and thus an even bigger danger.

So, where does that leave an agility practitioner?

Should she stay focused on changing her ways to craft better software and write elegant bug-free code, never mind that all that productivity will evaporate when it comes to the big picture?

Should the old manager relinquish "control" of the power he had worked so hard for, and become a facilitator or a coach just to be a more effective "servant leader," never mind that it could make him unmarketable for the industry at large?

---

[3]Just to illustrate the point, the average profit margins of S&P500 companies is in the range of 15-20%.

Should the traditional product manager simply become a curator of ideas crowdsourced from both inside and outside the team, without having his own say or expertise in how to go about building a kickass product?

Should the leader of the software organization "de-layer" the organization completely and adopt a more statesman-ish approach rather than leading the charge?

Should the customers change their expectations that a delivery team can't get a software right in case of "unknown-unknown" problems without them being involved and giving feedback every couple of weeks?

Before we dive deep into these question, let's go back in time and look at some ideas that exhibit agility before software industry rediscovered it.

Agility in Pre-software Days

In 1943, when WWII was at its peak, the US forces urgently needed a new jet fighter. Within a month of US Army's Air Tactical Service Command's (ATSC) meeting with Lockheed, a proposal was sent in June 1943. Work immediately started on it based on what was discussed over a handshake, never mind that the formal contract arrived only on Oct 16, by which time a solid four months of head start had already been gained. ATSC wanted the aircraft in 150 days. However, Lockheed, led by a young engineer, Kelly Johnson, delivered it in only 143 days.

What Kelly did is now better known as Skunk Works.[4] It is a great example of how best to remove obstacles and impediments to speed up the innovation and new product creation process.

Kelly's motto was "be quick, be quiet, be on time," and he formulated 14 principles and practices[5] to set up Skunk Works. Here's the complete list along with my commentary (in italics) on how I see it in the context of new product creation:

1. The Skunk Works manager must be delegated practically complete control of his program in all aspects. He should report to a division president or higher.

---

[4]Skunk Works Origin Story, www.lockheedmartin.co.in/us/aeronautics/skunkworks/origin.html.
[5]Kelly's 14 Rules and Practices, www.lockheedmartin.co.in/us/aeronautics/skunkworks/14rules.html. Reproduced with permission.

A new product development is fraught with several "unknown-unknowns" and, unlike a routine operations work such as sustaining or enhancements, it doesn't follow any predictable pattern. There will be lots of mistakes that often look like no progress is being made in a conventional sense, and, unless the team manager is given complete autonomy, decision-making and execution is likely to suffer. It only makes sense that the leader of the product team is given complete autonomy to run the program in the best possible manner. Any external interference is only likely to cause avoidable distractions.

2. Strong but small project offices must be provided both by the military and industry.

    We need to recognize that, in today's context, management is an overhead, and we must carefully limit the amount of managerial oversight required for a project. It must be commensurate to the kind of work being undertaken as well as the maturity of the team to handle such work. A small project office team will help ensure that the team is being given maximum autonomy to handle most of the issues by themselves and only the most critical issues are being addressed at project office level.

3. The number of people having any connection with the project must be restricted. Use a small number of good people (10–25% compared to the so-called normal systems).

    We can't overemphasize the need to have small teams. Large teams result in specializations, which tend to hide inefficiencies. The result is a dysfunctional team where delays in decision-making or finger-pointing in execution is far too common. As opposed, a small team knows they must collaborate with each other to deliver goods.

4. A very simple drawing and drawing release system with great flexibility for making changes must be provided.

    When you start a project with nothing but a handshake, you make a lot of assumptions about the system being developed. However, these assumptions must be validated in due course before irrecoverable investments are made. Validating the assumptions will invariably lead to subsequent changes that will help fine-tune the system specifications. If incorporating these changes requires complex decision-making and endless wait times and delays, the team is likely to lose momentum. Hence, it only makes sense to create a very lightweight and flexible system to incorporate changes.

5. There must be a minimum number of reports required, but important work must be recorded thoroughly.

   Kelly wanted to keep the administrative overhead to the bare minimum (how else could he promise to deliver the new plane in 150 days?), but make sure that key information was diligently captured. Often, status reports become a project unto themselves, taking far disproportionate amount of time and effort from the project manager (and his team) but hardly being "seen" by their intended audience.

6. There must be a monthly cost review covering not only what has been spent and committed but also what are projected costs to the conclusion of the program.

   While spending money against the budget is one of the critical measures of the health of the project, especially in capex-intensive projects, it is equally important to use that information to build projection into the future that allows the stakeholders to know what's happening in the trenches and respond appropriately.

7. The contractor must be delegated and must assume more than normal responsibility to get good vendor bids for subcontract on the project. Commercial bid procedures are very often better than military ones.

   When you are assigned responsibility for a project, you need to ensure that it is executed and delivered successfully. Quite often, we find that project managers are given accountability but don't have complete authority, which only ends up limiting their ability to influence the project.

8. The inspection system as currently used by the Skunk Works, which has been approved by both the Air Force and Navy, meets the intent of existing military requirements and should be used on new projects. Push more basic inspection responsibility back to subcontractors and vendors. Don't duplicate so much inspection.

   Who was being agile here? Kelly was shortening the feedback loop as close to the source of defect injection as possible. So, if there were subcontractors or vendors, he wanted them to inspect their work rather than Skunk Works to duplicate the inspection. A shorter feedback loop can help deliver a higher quality component, which in turn reduces the need for subsequent rework and can lead to faster execution and lowered costs of inspection and rework.

9.   The contractor must be delegated the authority to test his final product in flight. He can and must test it in the initial stages. If he doesn't, he rapidly loses his competency to design other vehicles.

Imagine if you are building several products and have no capability to test your product's key design in initial stages. Most likely, you will follow a similar process for all those products, and any mistakes made on one are likely to go unchecked and repeated in all other products that you build. An early inspection could help mitigate the risk of cascading a wrong process or a practice in all other products you build using a similar process.

10.   The specifications applying to the hardware must be agreed to well in advance of contracting. The Skunk Works practice of having a specification section stating clearly which important military specification items will not knowingly be complied with and reasons therefore is highly recommended.

In the past, hardware would not only constitute a major cost item, it would also have a significant time impact. Today, except for some very specialized systems, hardware is pretty much an off-the-shelf commodity. Businesses can simply rent a cloud and adjust its consumption on an on-demand basis.

11.   Funding a program must be timely so that the contractor doesn't have to keep running to the bank to support government projects.

While this might have been contextual to a private contractor servicing government projects, especially on time-critical new product development, it can be safely applied to just about anyone delivering bespoke products and services. If the contractor is not reimbursed in a timely manner for his products and services, focus from work will be redirected to finding a way to sustain his team, thereby losing track of the project priorities and commitments.

12.   There must be mutual trust between the military project organization and the contractor, the very close cooperation and liaison on a day-to-day basis. This cuts down misunderstanding and correspondence to an absolute minimum.

This seems like modern-day agile! In the middle of developing a complex, hi-tech product, Kelly is talking about trust as a key requirement. He clearly recognized that a new product development is an even bigger human endeavor, and there must be strong trust and collaboration on a daily basis to keep the flow going.

13. Access by outsiders to the project and its personnel must be strictly controlled by appropriate security measures.

    Surely this was in a military context, but it is relevant in commercial product development. The competition between market leaders is so intense that trade secrets and release schedules can have a major impact on the success of their future products.

14. Because only a few people will be used in engineering and most other areas, ways must be provided to reward good performance by pay not based on the number of personnel supervised.

    I think this is a great reminder why product companies exist and where most of IT/ITES services companies, and even some of the product companies, are going wrong.

So, what can we learn from how Kelly built a highly efficient and effective system of creating new products, especially in the context of building software products? I think most of these 14 rules apply quite well and could be a guide for anyone building new products, especially on a limited time budget. Now, let's examine the Agile Manifesto.

Re-examining the Agile Manifesto

The Agile Manifesto represents an event in time when some of the industry-leading practitioners pooled their ideas and experiences and built a common set of core values that represented their collective perspectives. Many of these ideas had been around for years before they became part of agile thinking. However, the Agile Manifesto succeeded in aligning them together so that practitioners could apply them in their work.

Following are the key events that happened before the Agile Manifesto came into existence:

- 1970: Royce *critiques* Waterfall and offers improvement ideas.

- 1971: Harlan Mills proposes Incremental Development.

- 1986: Barry Boehm proposes Spiral Model.

- 1986: The HBR article "The New New Product Development Game" comes onto the scene.
- 1987: Cleanroom software engineering is born.
- 1980s: Tom Gilb's Evo Project Management takes off.
- 1990: Peter DeGrace and Leslie Hulet Stahl publish *Wicked Problems, Righteous Solutions*, which introduces the concept of Scrum in software development based on "The New New Product Development Game".
- 1991: Sashimi Overlapping Waterfall Model is introduced.
- 1992: Crystal family of methodologies is embraced.
- 1994: DSDM is released.
- 1995: Jeff Sutherland and Ken Schwaber propose Scrum.
- 1996: Rational Unified Process framework debuted.
- 1997: Feature-Driven Development is introduced.
- 1999: *Extreme Programming Explained* is published.
- 2001: The Agile Manifesto is born.

Of course, the signing of the Agile Manifesto was only one of the many events preceding and succeeding the movement. For example, the major events that continue to evolve post-Agile Manifesto include the following:

- 2003: May Poppendeick publishes *Lean Software Development.*
- 2005: PM Declaration of Interdependence is created.
- 2005: Steve Blank introduces Customer Development methodology in *Four Steps to the Epiphany.*
- 2008: Eric Ries introduces the Lean Startup approach.
- 2009: Scrumban methodology is introduced.
- 2010: David Anderson publishes *Kanban.*
- 2011: Corey Ladas publishes *Scrumban.*
- 2011: Alexander Osterwalder publishes *Business Model Generation.*

As we can see, the journey to agility has been a long one and most of its underlying principles have been around for more than a few decades. Unfortunately, it still continues to surprise and shock that most people think these are new-age software development methods, and tend to disregard them with contempt. Perhaps a discussion about its principles is in order.

The Agile Manifesto

The notion of agility in software development is well-documented in the Agile Manifesto (http://agilemanifesto.org). In 2001, 17 leading practitioners of alternate software methods met at a ski resort in Utah and came up with the following manifesto:

MANIFESTO FOR AGILE SOFTWARE DEVELOPMENT

We are uncovering better ways of developing software by doing it and helping others do it.

Through this work we have come to value:

Individuals and interactions *over processes and tools*

Working software *over comprehensive documentation*

Customer collaboration *over contract negotiation*

Responding to change *over following a plan*

That is, while there is value in the items on the right, we value the items on the left more.

Kent Beck	James Grenning	Robert C. Martin
Mike Beedle	Jim Highsmith	Steve Mellor
Arie van Bennekum	Andrew Hunt	Ken Schwaber
Alistair Cockburn	Ron Jeffries	Jeff Sutherland
Ward Cunningham	Jon Kern	Dave Thomas
Martin Fowler	Brian Marick	

© 2001, the above authors

This declaration may be freely copied in any form, but only in its entirety through this notice.

The authors were disappointed with the state of practice at that time. They didn't see how frameworks like Software CMM, standards like ISO9000, or the numerous tools that were beginning to mushroom all over the place were going to solve the problem of software development.

The Agile Manifesto was perhaps the earliest attempt to come from practitioners' community as opposed from a standards body of upper- management consultants. Perhaps this is the reason it was not taken seriously in its initial years, despite its intuitive appeal at an individual and a team level. Undoubtedly, it left several questions unanswered, especially those pertaining to outside the agile teams: How does the agile team operate in the context of a large organization? What is the role of leadership? What is the notion of agility outside the software team? How do you organize a large and distributed team?

How do you organize an R&D team? These questions were all very pertinent with no immediate answers, at least not ones that could convince the change sponsors to try them out.

However, despite these known issues, the set of four core values and twelve principles supporting the manifesto gave a solid framework for agile teams to operate with high efficiency and efficacy. By itself, it didn't alter any management hierarchy or power structures. Nonetheless, it was not received very positively. Steve Denning calls Agile the best-kept secret in management today[6] and feels management continues to live in denial about it, with the most prestigious Harvard Business Review hardly mentioning "…even an oblique reference to the solution that Agile offers to one of the fundamental management problems of our times."

Even though management continues to live in denial mode, let's examine how we as software development community responded to some of these ideas.

Are you serving the process well?

On one hand, we have this large industry of trainers, certification factories, coaches, consultants, and process methodologists who all bring their pet version of yoga promising to cure all chronic maladies.[7] In several cases, certainly much more than what I'd like to see, they "teach" a process that they claim is *the* agile way. And yes, the big bold (marketing) disclaimer that often goes with it—you must follow the process in entirety, or else it becomes "agile-but,"[8] as if being "agile-but" is the most heinous crime of them all! In most of these cases, the method evangelists literally make you feel that following the process is why software teams exist in the first place.

Can we skip this practice?

Nope, you can't do that.

OK, how about using another technique that we have been following and seems to work reasonably well for us?

No way, that is waterfall!

I like this practice from the other agile process. Can I blend it in?

I don't know what you are talking about!

---

[6]www.forbes.com/sites/stevedenning/2012/04/09/the-best-kept-management-secret-on-the-planet-agile/.

[7]Some of us have seen this script play a couple times before as well. In the 1980s, it was TQM, SPC, and BPR; in the 1990s, it was CMM, Six Sigma, and ISO9000. Thankfully, we haven't found the silver bullet yet.

[8]I have used "agile-but" in a generic sense to represent the viewpoint that quite often people claim they are applying the agile method, but they don't follow all its guidelines. While I agree with the intent behind this viewpoint, it suggests that there is only right way to being agile.

I see a major challenge with this narrow and self-serving thinking. We are forever confusing the means with the ends. Let's step back and understand why are we even developing software in the first place.

In my mind, a business exists to make ethical profits in a sustainable manner, whatever profits those might be—providing a return to shareholders, providing cleantech, enriching the lives of disadvantaged communities, having happy employees, and so on. Hence, there is no such things as a true non-profit. Now, over a period of time, businesses go through cycles of growth, stagnation, and slowdowns. They face a constant barrage of ever-increasing competition, globalization, lowering prices, decreasing customer loyalty, ever-increasing customer expectations and demands, trade barriers, and so forth. Several businesses simply pack up. The company size doesn't seem to matter. Standard and Poor's 500 index replaces over two dozen companies each year, which averages to one company among the largest 500 companies on NYSE and NASDAQ every fortnight. On the other hand, over 90% of the startups fail. Irrespective of the process these business follow, could you call them agile? Nokia was a great poster child of agile adoption, but when the company was left fighting for survival on the "burning platform",[9] it didn't seem to make a great story about it being agile. Yahoo! has been a great company and a big champion of agile development, but if you look at its topline and bottom-line for the last 5+ years, it has largely remained flat. Would we consider these success stories in their agile adoption journeys?

On the other hand, the best businesses often come out of these cycles stronger, resilient, efficient, and innovative. To that end, a business that is constantly growing and getting better at its game is already "agile," no matter what brand of agile it follows. How does that even matter? Such businesses have learned, and some have even mastered, the art, science, management, and leadership of what it takes to survive in the real world. And just like no two problems are alike, these businesses recognize that adapting to the situations in real time is key to success, much like their biological equivalent. Taking Darwin's premise, we can safely say that for today's businesses, adaptation is key. Process is secondary. And the specific flavor of process is a distant tertiary.

And what is adaptation all about? When we say organizations need to be adaptable, we are not talking about the building and furniture being adaptable to business cycles! We are talking about the individuals that constitute an organization—whatever roles they might be playing. So, in the end, it is all about people.

---

[9]http://blogs.wsj.com/tech-europe/2011/02/09/full-text-nokia-ceo-stephen-elops-burning-platform-memo/.

Unfortunately, in our zeal, we often forget that it is people who created process and that the processes are meant to serve people—not the other way round. What will a group of reasonably intelligent people do in the absence of a process? If all they will do it wait for an epiphany or instructions or a catastrophe, then have we failed to give them a thinking process?

True agility is not about following a great "agile process," but having the right set of people collaborate and figure out their own way of working. When situations change, as they eventually will, this group finds the best way to adapt to the evolving situation.

If an agile process ever exists in reality, its only indicator of existence must be that it changes every now and then!

Tools can't be wrong!

An equally strong industry of toolmakers promise the moon through their tools, never mind that agility is fundamentally all about people. Surely, the tool movement is not new. When I was doing my masters in the late 1980s, the new big thing on the horizon was the so-called CASE tools, or Computer Aided Software Engineering. The grand promise was that if only we could somehow specify all the requirements, we might develop the software "faster, better, cheaper." The CASE tool movement died, but the dream didn't. In the 1990s, there were toolmakers who would claim that if you bought their tools, you would get "CMM Level 3" out of the box—whatever that meant!

So, where does that leave a practitioner? They refer to the Agile Manifesto only to learn that the first value states the following:

Individuals and Interactions *over process and tools*

They question if individuals and interactions is indeed the bedrock of agile software development, why are we insisting and enforcing one particular brand of agile? Should it not be left to those individuals to figure out their own process and decide what tool they want to use? Are the process and tools meant for CEO, the VPs, and the procurement team, or the engineers in the trenches? In most cases, senior leadership is not prepared to answer these questions honestly.

What happens inside a team is far more important than institutionalized processes that might have no context to the team's local dynamics. Most organizations and leaders fail to recognize this aspect and find ways to enforce an institutionalized way to run projects, and track and report project progress. Not only is this single-minded approach reminiscent of the old industrial way of doing software development, it also serves no particular purpose. If upper management is looking for some specific ways to get the information, let them negotiate with the managers or the product owner and the scrum master (or their equivalent in non-scrum teams). But for goodness sake, don't use the production-era process-thinking to solve a problem that doesn't exist in the knowledge-era new-product development thinking.

Customers are human beings too!

When a customer contracts us to build something, it is tempting to ask them for all the minutest details and plan accordingly. If we are able to deliver them all, we can delight our customers. Sounds simple and easy, right?

Wrong!

Let's go back again to the Stacey Matrix. When we are solving the simple class of problems, it is relatively easy to identify all the variables in a project.[10] If you can specify all the variables, you can ask someone else to do the project for you. The only source of uncertainty is the normal causes of process variance and the contractor's ability to execute to the plan. Assuming you have found the right vendor, it would be safe to say that if you could build a solid contract, you could be finished. Sadly, software development—especially in new-product creation—isn't often like that. It is more in the complex or complicated or even anarchy zone. Thus, drafting a contract when so many variables are unknown is not just detrimental to the contractor's commercial interests, it is equally, or more, dangerous for the customer. For the contractor, a project gone awry might only be only a loss of name and money, but for a customer, it might be loss of real market opportunity.

So, what is the best way to deal with contractual relationships when there are several variables in the equation? The Agile Manifesto's third value is all about creating a collaborative relationship with the customer as opposed to a strict customer-vendor relationship only dictated by the contract:

Customer collaboration *over contract negotiation*

Obviously, it is easier said than done! Not all customers will understand the importance of collaboration. If they happen to talk to their legal folks, there is no chance they are ever going to get advice that favors a collaborative approach over a contractual one, especially if you are working with a large company that will eventually seek to indemnify them against any potential damages due to poor quality or incorrect implementation. Fair enough.

However, if we go a bit deeper to understand the sources of such poor quality or incorrect implementation, we might be able to attribute them to the fundamental nature of software being a "wicked problem."

---

[10]One might argue that it is never easy to outsource, and I don't disagree with that. My point is that with everything else being equal, it is still be easier to outsource a simple problem than to ask someone else to build a complex system for us.

In 1973, Horst Rittel and Melvin Webber introduced the concept of wicked problem in their treatise "Dilemmas in a General Theory of Planning"[11] and propounded that planning problems are inherently "wicked". They defined wicked problems as basically problems that were complex and had no simple solution. They also identified ten characteristics of a wicked problem:

1. There is definite formulation of a wicked problem.

2. Wicked problems have no stopping rule.

3. Solutions to wicked problems are not true-or-false, but good-or-bad.

4. There is no immediate and no ultimate test of a solution to a wicked problem.

5. Every solution to a wicked problem is a "one shot operation"; because there is no opportunity to learn by trial-and-error, every attempt counts significantly.

6. Wicked problems do not have an enumerable (or an exhaustively describable) set of potential solutions, nor is there a well-described set of permissible operations that may be incorporated into the plan.

7. Every wicked problem is essentially unique.

8. Every wicked problem can be considered to be a symptom of another problem.

9. The existence of a discrepancy representing a wicked problem can be explained in numerous ways. The choice of explanation determines the nature of the problem's resolution.

10. The planner has no right to be wrong.

While their original idea of wicked problems pertained to social problems, the idea was soon picked up to describe problems in several domains, including software development. Several of these characteristics apply extremely well to software development.

---

[11]www.uctc.net/mwebber/Rittel+Webber+Dilemmas+General_Theory_of_Planning.pdf.

In 1990, Peter deGrace and Leslie Hulet Stahl wrote *Wicked Problems, Righteous Solutions*, which, perhaps, for the first time recognized that software development was more like a wicked problem. Regarding the title of their book, they said, "The title of the book reflects, I'm sorry to say, a condition of our field where there are often more moral issues than technical ones. That is why I have chosen the term 'wicked' to describe a certain set of problems that involve not only large and complex problems of a technical nature, but also problems of a moral nature. This book provides some righteous solutions to these wicked problems." How do they suggest solving wicked problems? Here are some excerpts from the book that help us understand their viewpoint:

> "…the problem is fully understood only after it is solved. This means that intermediate results must be obtained before a final solution can be reached, or that a problem is defined and solved at the same time."

They introduce the analogy with successive approximation in engineering as the way to produce a solution. They also offer a similar way to solve a market problem in software product development:

> … there is a similar procedure in the consumer software market. We produce a word processor, take it to the market, and wait for the feedback, which provides the initial results. This feedback is in the form of revenue, product reviews, complaints, and suggestions. It tells us whether or not we have at least partially solved the problem of producing an acceptable word processor … My correspondents in the consumer market tell me that although they start off with a "specification," they do not maintain it. It is a "seed" document, and the current specifications are in the source code of the product.

They consider using waterfall ineffective for solving these "untameable" problems because it is difficult to make waterfall iterate, and it must be based on a complete set of unambiguous requirements. If we concede that software development is indeed a wicked problem, it sounds like a logical fallacy that its full specifications can ever be known, most certainly never known in the beginning of the project. This implies that any form of writing down the contract sounds like wishful thinking and potentially open for misinterpretation.

The authors of the Agile Manifesto advised not attempting to solve the unsolvable by using the waterfall approach of "specifying" the requirements upfront, but gradually learning about them by close collaboration with the customer.

Show, don't tell!

When computers were introduced more than 50 years ago, they were extremely costly and, as a result, very rare. If you had to use a computer, you had to book the time, which would be costly in terms of money and often wasteful in terms of time.

When I was growing up in the beautiful city of Udaipur, my father was pursuing his PhD in nuclear physics. The mainframes closest to Udaipur were in National Physical Lab Ahmedabad or IIT Delhi. He would typically go there once every few months, with a bagful of punch cards, and run his programs and then come back to work on the data further. If he made a mistake during that time, he would lose a few months of work time.

When I was earning my master's in computer science in 1989, we had a Russian mainframe in the college, an EC1045. It had only six terminals, and over 150+ students in various courses would have to wait for their turn to use it (or they could just use the MS-DOS based IBM PC/XT/AT, but those were also shared resources in the computer lab). For the mainframe, we would typically be allotted an hour per week. So, I would sit on the (dumb) terminal and starting punching in my FORTRAN or COBOL program. I had only one hour to not only type my code, but also to compile it, debug it, test it, and finally take printout for the lab assignment. One hour would never be enough, but if the work were not completed, I would have to wait for one more week and sometimes miss the assignment deadline. So, our professors would insist on the age-old way to address it—measure twice, cut one. We would be required to write down the pseudo code, perform a dry run, write the code and manually test it, do the boundary value partitioning, do the static code analysis, and so on … all on paper! We would spend hours just getting to an error-free code before we could sit in front of the terminal and write it! Why? Because the machine time was much costlier compared to the programmer time.

When I started working in the 1990s, the process movement had taken over, and documentation had become like an organized religion. Unfortunately, it not only took too much time to document things, it also failed to provide remedies for the reason it was created—feedback on the workmanship of the product. For example, looking at an MS Word document or even a UML diagram, there was no way to know if certain performance criteria could actually be met until that code was actually written. So, it was solving a problem that didn't quite exist. Upper management as well as the customers was sure that the project was proceeding well because they had documents to show it, and the team had no other option.

Over time, thanks to Moore's law and mass production, the prices of machines kept getting lower while the programmer salaries continued to rise. The economics of software development had reversed—it was much cheaper to get an hour of computing time than an hour of programmer time. And thanks to the availability of cheap and smart tools, programmers could continue to tinker around with code and debug it without worrying about old economics.

It made much more sense to simply write software and show it than to write reams of documentation, which supports the following agile value:

Working software *over comprehensive documentation*

Today, it is almost unthinkable that someone will first take weeks or months to write meaningless documentation and then get it reviewed and approved before starting to write code. Today's businesses and customers don't have that kind of time.

Google's AdWords program is the main source of Google's advertising revenue. It was revamped as a weekend project.[12] Imagine trying to write documentation to first show how it works!

I'm loving it!

When we were planning to build our house, my wife and I engaged with an architect. We basically gave him a lowdown of what we had in mind, and he said he would come back with a design in a couple of weeks. When he shared his designs, we liked some aspects but didn't like others. We asked the architect to make changes that we wanted—not that he wanted. The conversations weren't always easy, and finally getting to something that we could all agree upon took more than a dozen iterations and perhaps an entire quarter. Why is it that once we create something, we fall in love with our creation and don't like any changes to it, even if that happens to come from our customers who are paying for it and are the ones who are actually going to use it?

We seek comfort in the plans we make, and any slightest variation is seen as most unwelcome! Give a set of Lego blocks to a child and let her build something. After she has built something that she adores, ask her to make some changes. Chances are that you will be talking to one very stubborn child. Ask a project manager to make changes to his plans or ask an architect to make changes to her design, and you are almost guaranteed to be given a lesson in software design!

We think the best thing after building a plan is to follow the plan, lest we be faulted on poor execution. Unfortunately, life is not that simple. Not only do our customers want change, but when they ask for change, it is actually great news. It shows they care for the product and want suitable changes to make the product more usable to them. Keeping this in mind, the Agile Manifesto signatories proposed the following value:

Responding to change *over following a plan*

Of course, it is easier said than done! A lot of customers expect us to make good on our commitments! Once we tell them our plans, they want us to stick to the plans, for no one likes surprises. But, what if halfway through the project,

---

[12]www.newyorker.com/magazine/2014/12/01/g-m-google.

the technology changes, or a new competitor comes up with some really cool features, or the government changes laws that make your plans worthless, or just about any other external factor that could essentially render sticking to your plans useless? What are you going to do? If you want to stick to the original plans, you might learn, much to your dismay, that there isn't a market or a customer for it, no matter how much you pat yourself for on-time and on-budget completion of the project. A far more pragmatic way would be to recognize that by asking you to incorporate those late changes, the customer is actually giving you a great chance to stay relevant in the business.

Accelerating the Agility

These four core values lay the foundation for agility in software development. However, agility is not a single-point outcome, but it must be deliberately practiced and applied at multiple levels—right from individual, team, organization, and business levels for true agility to be achieved and sustained. I call this accelerating the agility.

Software development is a social sport. We bring individuals to the table, and then, based on whom are we playing against, we pick up the team that best represents our chances of winning. If a project requires lots of complicated algorithms, we might need some strong computer science grads or, more recently, the data scientists. If the work requires building some cool user experience, we might need some eccentric designers (yes, that's right, because they tend to be really sharp and worth the money they command). Of course, a lot of work just requires a focused and flawless execution, in which case, we require people who can sustain a pre-defined process over a long period of time while making incremental progress in execution performance.

However, life is not always as compartmentalized as this, and neither is the talent.

Products are born when a crazy new idea is born. We get literally hundreds of ideas daily. Certainly not all of them are the game-changers of tomorrow. Referring back to the Stacey Matrix, the new ideas are typically "unknown-unknowns" and require a thinking framework to build hypotheses; test them using minimum amounts of time, effort, and money; and then quickly learn before your competitors do.

At an individual level, it requires creating an environment that empowers and motivates individuals to not just deliver their best but also to go over and above their assigned roles and responsibilities to search for better solutions. If team members have to wait for hours or days for small clarifications or decisions, they don't just lose time and productivity, they also lose the motivation and commitment to perform the task. Eliminating hierarchy so that team members can directly decide which tasks to work on, how best to organize the work, when to contact the customer directly, and where to get early and frequent feedback is one way we can accelerate the individual agility. In addition, the engineering practices such as practicing test-driven development, refactoring, test automation, continuous integration, and pair programming are some of the great ways to reduce length and cost of the feedback loop, thus making an engineer much more efficient (how best to do something), focused (what to work on), empowered (how to solve a given problem), committed (why we are doing it), and effective (how we are delivering the right value to the customer).

At the team level, not only do the members need the support and resources, they also need a management system that allows them to select work that they can deliver proudly in a sustainable manner. When they serve only one master (for example, listen only to the product owner in a scrum team), their work creates the highest value for its customers. When they are allowed to make team-level commitments, it raises the team trust to unprecedented heights and allows them to self-organize to solve any kind of unplanned or unforeseen problems. A team's agility has two dimensions—internal and external. Internal dimension means that when a team is stuck and its commitments are in jeopardy, the members are allowed to look inwards and find the best possible solution. External dimension means that when the customer requires changes in deliverables, the customer is able to engage with the team without going through multiple layers of hierarchy and negotiate a win-win solution.

At the organizational level, being agile determines how fast an organization is able to capitalize on the market opportunities. In the Skunk Works example, Lockheed didn't wait to get a formal purchase order. Indeed, by the time it got the formal work order, he and his team had already completed four months of work—which was roughly 80% of the schedule on a time-critical project of global geopolitical significance.

And, finally, there is the issue of agility at the business level. I would typically look at bottom-line, cash cycle, and the "inventory turns" as three critical metrics that tell me how efficient you are as a business, how fast you convert raw materials into revenues, and how many times you are able to do it in a year.

Guess what the average profits of S&P500 index companies are? In 2014, the average profit margin was 9.5%—which is 61% highest since 1980.[13] In 2012, the net margins varied from 2.9% for food and staples retailing to 20.2% for software and services. Let's just concentrate on the software sector. If the best companies only manage to make 20% profits, why don't all the fancy claims of productivity improvements at team level to the tune of 400% or 1,000% quite add up? Doesn't it raise a few questions about the true effectiveness of business agility?

---

[13]www.forbes.com/sites/janetnovack/2014/10/28/profit-peril-sp-500-margins-are-near-multi-decade-high/.

Let's look at cash cycle. The best businesses have negative cash cycles—they make money from their customers even before they pay their suppliers. Some of the famous examples include Toyota, Amazon (-30.6 days in 2013)[14], Apple (-44.5 days in 2013).

In terms of inventory turns, it is a great measure of business agility. It essentially means how many times a business is able to sell its inventory in a given time period. The higher, the better. Typical manufacturing companies might do 6–8 turns per year; Samsung does 17, while Dell does 36. However, Apple leads with 74 inventory turns a year, or almost selling its entire inventory every 5 days,[15] indeed a great indicator of how well its products sell and how lean its own inventory is.

When your business is that agile, does it matter what name you give to your process?

What's next?

Jim Highsmith wrote[16] a very interesting behind-the-scenes account of what happened before the Agile Manifesto was crafted. Among other things, one of the interesting thoughts shared goes like this:

> The Agile Movement is not anti-methodology, in fact, many of us want to restore credibility to the word "methodology." We want to restore a balance. We embrace modeling, but not in order to file some diagram in a dusty corporate repository. We embrace documentation, but not hundreds of pages of never-maintained and rarely used tomes. We plan, but recognize the limits of planning in a turbulent environment.

I think it is important to recognize that the agile movement is not just about a new process. It is a new management system for the knowledge industry, and perhaps the first one that recognizes that people are far more important than processes or systems.

In this book, we will examine how we apply principles of agility to accomplish our business goals in a more effective manner than in the past. We will discuss various approaches as we take an idea and build it into a tangible product.

Welcome to the beautiful world of Agile Product Development.

---

[14]https://hbr.org/2014/10/at-amazon-its-all-about-cash-flow/.
[15]www.theatlantic.com/technology/archive/2012/05/wow-apple-turns-over-its-inventory-once-every-5-days/257915/.
[16]History: The Agile Manifesto, http://agilemanifesto.org/history.html.

Discover

Let's find the next big idea

Discovery consists of seeing what everybody has seen, and thinking what nobody has thought.

—Albert Szent-Gyorgyi

In the beginning, it was all about accidental discovery.

Who first discovered how to start a fire? We don't know who, but we know that humans have used fire since the early Stone Age. Who invented the wheel? Again, we don't know who, but the wheel has been around for more than five thousand years.

When we examine these technological breakthroughs closely, we ask, "Were they simply accidental discoveries or were they the result of deliberate efforts?" If consider them accidents, we don't seem to be giving much credit to the brainpower of mankind. If these were accidents, what facilitated them? Do we observe a direct correlation between the environmental conditions, and the quantity and quality of such accidents? The accident theory seems limiting. If we still rely on the power of accidents for the growth of mankind, then why do we fund research and development? Perhaps we should stop pumping in all those dollars into so-called research and simply let people experiment haphazardly, and hopefully something interesting will eventually emerge.

The twentieth century was all about funding huge research labs in order to build engines of innovation. In addition, companies would run large market research campaigns to learn about customer behavior so that product development could keep up with customer preferences. This model worked well in the pre-Internet era of mass production and trade barriers. With a more globalized knowledge economy, products and services enabled by the Internet began to mushroom all over the world and brought in a new system of discovering the next big idea quickly—that is, one of experimenting and gradually refining the idea. Companies that barely existed five years ago are today's multibillion-dollar cap companies. Companies such as Google that are still celebrating their teenage years are buying grandfather companies like Motorola. Clearly, the rules of product discovery have changed over time, and the larger and established companies are increasingly finding themselves out of their depth in a world dominated by the fast pace of technology adoption and the equally fast pace of technology obsolescence. The old methods of elaborate market research, followed by multiyear cycles of product development are just not effective anymore. And the new methods of product discovery seem to be founded more on the accidental discovery type of paradigm rather than some kind of purposeful innovation. How else do you explain an idea like WhatsApp or Snapchat taking over the online world by storm? Could they have been come to fruition with such long-haul methods?

So, what is the answer? I think while serendipity plays a great role in discovery of knowledge, there is the human brain plays a far greater role—without the power of the human brain, we would perhaps fail to even recognize serendipity. And if there is a method to the madness, what is it—are there tools and techniques that could be used to stimulate and channelize human creativity into a tangible solution? Or, are we simply dependent on the lone genius as opposed to a team working on a problem?

Let's examine some of the key patterns that have evolved in the last few decades:

Accidental Discovery vs. Directed Innovation

The phenomenon of making technological breakthroughs accidentally seems to be getting rarer. While Archimedes perhaps "accidentally" discovered buoyancy while taking a bath and Newton famously "discovered" gravity while sitting under an apple tree, the serendipitous nature of scientific discoveries seems to have peaked 150 years ago. Penicillin, the microwave oven, Velcro, Teflon, vulcanized rubber, Coca-Cola, Post-its, radioactivity, smart dust, saccharin, the slinky, Play-Doh, super glue, Bakelite … even potato chips, stainless steel, and Viagra … are examples of "accidental" discoveries and inventions. However, when we examine the first 15 years of the twenty-first century, many discoveries aren't being attributed to accidents and chance— rather they are more and more purposeful, even if their starting point was not as promising as the discoveries themselves eventually ended up being.

Indeed in many cases, accidental discoveries did not go on to become overnight successes. When Dr. Spencer Silver, a scientist at 3M, discovered a low-quality glue in 1968, he spent years trying to promote it internally within 3M before running into another scientist, Art Fry, in 1973, after which 3M decided to mass produce Post-it notes. However, the product was not exactly a runaway success, and it failed to attract consumer interest when launched as "Press 'n Peel" in four cities in 1977. The product didn't take off until 3M implemented a different strategy. In 1980, 3M released the product onto the national market by issuing free samples directly to customers—a whopping 94% of those who tried the product indicated interest in buying the product. We are often intrigued by the "overnight success" stories, but even brilliant ideas such as Post-it notes had to struggle through 12 years of trials and tribulations before market launch!

On other side of the spectrum, elaborate and extensive research was not able to save such great companies as Kodak, Motorola, Radio Shack, and Polaroid. Such research also didn't lead to the success of Microsoft Zune or HP's tablet or Amazon's Fire smartphone.

Hence, if you are a company or a startup intending to introduce the next big idea quickly, what is your best bet—take a gut-feeling approach and start experimenting until an accidental discovery happens; or pump in time, effort, and money to find that perfect market opportunity, never mind that by the time you get to launch it, the market might have moved on?

I think neither of these extremes makes sense in today's world. While accidental discovery might be possible, business plans can't be built around a team of bright individuals waiting and hoping for a miracle to happen. Similarly, large-scale, directed innovation might not be possible for lean-and-mean-startups that barely have the money to survive beyond next few months.

We clearly need methods that allow for discovering the next killer idea in a more directed manner that could be done on a shoestring budget in a short amount of time.

Lone Genius vs. Cross-Functional Team

The idea of a lone genius is a timeless, romantic one. It appeals to the human heart and emotions more than to the brain and the rational mind. It is also a convenient way to rationalize successes—of course, the creator had born talent, and lesser mortals simply didn't have what it took to create things or build stuff!

The lone genius metaphor is now mostly replaced with the idea of a cross-functional team whose members complement each other with their individual strengths, allowing the team to make better decisions and move much more rapidly than simply relying on a single brain. Leonardo da Vinci did not lock himself up in a corner and come up with those fantastic ideas all by himself. Instead, as a member of a vibrant community established by the Medici family at the Garden of the Piazza San Marco in Florence, he collaborated with other luminaries of his time. Isaac Newton graciously said, "If I have seen further, it is by standing on the shoulders of giants," referring to the works of countless others before him upon which he was able to develop his own work.

The Jan 30, 2012, issue of *The New Yorker* published an interesting article titled "Groupthink: The Brainstorming myth."[1] There is an interesting bit of data from the article:

> ... Ben Jones, a professor at the Kellogg School of Management, at Northwestern University, has quantified this trend. By analyzing 19.9 million peer-reviewed academic papers and 2.1 million patents from the past fifty years, he has shown that levels of teamwork have increased in more than ninety-five per cent of scientific subfields; the size of the average team has increased by about twenty per cent each decade. The most frequently cited studies in a field used to be the product of a lone genius, like Einstein or Darwin. Today, regardless of whether researchers are studying particle physics or human genetics, science papers by multiple authors receive more than twice as many citations as those by individuals. This trend was even more apparent when it came to so-called "home-run papers"—publications with at least a hundred citations. These were more than six times as likely to come from a team of scientists.

This is an interesting observation—backed by solid research and data—.that flies in the face of the "lone genius myth" There is enough data to suggest that we are facing more and more complex problems than what a single human mind can individually comprehend, and perhaps cross-functional problems need multiple specialists to collaborate more than ever before.

A key aspect of a cross-functional team is in its flexibility and adaptability. Problems never remain static, and invariably the team working on it must change its tactics and experiment with multiple approaches. In the agile world, a cross-functional team allows for thinking on a problem completely "vertically", that is, from the top of a customer's touch point down to the entire tech stack. This creates customer value as opposed to simply delivering horizontal

---

[1] www.newyorker.com/magazine/2012/01/30/groupthink?currentPage=all

layers of partial software functionality that neither solve a customer's pain point nor allow the development team to validate any key hypotheses or make any tangible progress.

Indeed, in many cases, the team might have to start all over again, and solve a totally different problem than first anticipated. Agile takes the idea of a cross-functional team to a "self-organizing team" which doesn't stay in its silos, but is willing to adapt itself and acquire newer competencies to handle emergent problems more effectively. A self-organizing team has a very high team-chemistry environment where trust replaces controls, and curiosity replaces fear—even failures are rewards as they eventually lead to better results. When challenged with a problem that it has never faced before, a self-organizing team doesn't express its helplessness in its inability to solve the problem. Instead, it regroups itself, quickly finds the key gaps, and works coherently to fill the gaps. It recognizes that the confidence and power of a team comes from the ability and willingness to continuously learn new things. No problem is too big for a self-organizing team.

Slow Market Research vs. Rapid Experimentation

The erstwhile market research is increasingly being seen as a too long-drawn-out and rigid process to build products and services in a dynamic world with increasingly short technology adoption cycles. We need to remember that while it took 75 years for the telephone to reach 50 million users and the radio 38 years, it only took 3.5 years for Facebook to reach that mark, and for Angry Birds, it was just 35 days. What level of market research can you do to compete in this market? The rather slow-moving process of yesteryears might favor rigorous elaboration and testing of all the steps that lead to launching a new product, but the market opportunity might be over by the time that happens, thus rendering those efforts completely useless. Clearly, we need to upgrade our methods.

The new-age entrepreneurs, armed with methods like Design Thinking and Lean Startups, don't have the patience or the budget to fund elaborate, multiyear market research. They would much rather take an initial hypothesis and quickly design experiments to validate it in a so-called "fail fast, fail cheap, fall forward" manner. If the experiment "fails," it is celebrated as a success because it allowed us to quickly validate a key assumption and saved us precious time and money from a certain wild goose chase.[2] More importantly,

---

[2]Check out this interesting video on how $40 saved a startup $2million and 9 months of effort: https://vimeo.com/24749599

it allowed us to "pivot" our plans much sooner (that is, change the strategy without changing the vision, and increase the odds of eventual success by making a series of course-corrections while it was still easier and cheaper to do so). However, being able to operate at that level requires a fundamentally different thinking than is unfortunately available in most organizations, especially those with a glorious and successful past. Take Sony. It was successful in Trinitron technology and was the market leader. This success stopped them from exploring flat-screen TVs, eventually causing them to almost lose the plasma and LCD market. Other examples include Sony Walkman's inability to lead the innovation into digital music and Kodak's reluctance to move from chemistry to digital photos.

When Yahoo! launched BOSS—Build Your Own Search Service—in 2008, developers were able to actually build something and use that for experimentation to learn about what customers might need from a search engine instead of using a focus-group survey to elicit requirements. I have heard of people using BOSS to build a search engine in four hours flat. However, when I was writing this chapter, I saw an interesting new item in my Facebook's news feed—a developer built a Facebook messenger app for Windows in a whopping three minutes[3] flat! Whether these ideas survive beyond the initial euphoria or even the "1.0" avatar, is immaterial. What they do is of tremendous value because they allow potential users to play around with the ideas and share meaningful feedback back to developers.

In the world of idea discovery, there are no guarantees or set formulas for success We must experiment to learn more about a problem. However, experiments that take several years and consume millions of dollars are not the best approach in today's world. First off, no one might have that luxury. Secondly, even if the results are proven successful, by the time a development team uses those results and creates products based on those results, the market might have moved on, thereby rendering such efforts completely useless. A team must find a way to learn in short baby steps by a series of rapid experiments. Learning can simply not be a one-time event, but rather a continuous process.

Role-Based Innovation vs. Ability-Based Innovation

Traditional organizations have hierarchies, functional boundaries, and roles that decide who can innovate and who can't. Corporate syndromes like NIH ("Not Invented Here") limit the inflow of new ideas because the incumbents

---

[3]http://venturebeat.com/2015/04/09/watch-this-developer-build-a-facebook-messenger-app-for-windows-in-3-minutes/

feel threatened that others are encroaching upon their boundaries. I am not an expert enough historian to judge whether it worked in the past, but I do know that such a model is not likely to work today (and I can fairly well guess that people must have hated it even back then!). The young workforce in knowledge industry is looking at a level playing field where they are not simply there to spin their wheels, but be heard and given the opportunity to bring change. Unfortunately, a lot of the old guard is not willing to listen. They still believe that innovation is what separates leaders from workers.

Could innovation be democratized? Yes, absolutely. Should innovation be democratized? No doubt! In today's world, it is a criminal waste of human talent to stop individuals from improving the company. Having seen the power of young minds, I have no doubt that organizations that fail to democratize innovation will soon find their best minds walking away, either to their competition or, worse, creating startups their own. And those left inside the system will either be people who have simply learned to abide by rules of survival (which means, not to open up their mouths) or those left with no new ideas to contribute. Either way, those organizations stand to lose in the face of a globalized flat and increasingly VUCA[4] world—volatile, uncertain, complex and ambiguous. Given that S&P 500 index replaces one among the 500 largest companies by market cap every two weeks, I think there are no guarantees that any company of any size will survive if it can't keep pace with the fast-evolving future.

Ideas and Techniques

In this section, we will discuss ideas and techniques that you and your team could utilize to discover the next big idea quickly. Like every good technique, there are areas where it works well while, but in other environments, other methods and techniques might be better suited. While it might be foolhardy to master one or two techniques and apply them in all situations and expect equally stellar results, it might be equally useless to be familiar with all the methods without really knowing when or why to choose one over other. We will also discuss how each of these techniques differs from each other and when are they likely to be most useful.

Let's examine if some of the ideation methods can help us mitigate the risks of homeostasis.

---

[4]What VUCA Really Means for you, https://hbr.org/2014/01/what-vuca-really-means-for-you

Brainstorming

It is easier to tone down a wild idea than to think up a new one.

—Alex Osborne

Imagine participating in a meeting where the atmosphere is highly politically charged. There are rival factions that are out to nix any new ideas from opposing camps. Then there are self-appointed perennial naysayers (and old-school and agenda-less critics) who believe their only job is to protect the organization against "those crazy new ideas." Of course, there are leaders who like to show that they value everyone's opinions, but actually want their own ideas to be in the ones in place. And then, finally, you have the lowly employees who are being told that their ideas are valued, but with hardly any realistic opportunity of sharing their ideas. Can you guess how many new, bold, and creative ideas are likely to come out of such a meeting? While this might seem straight out of Dilbert comics, an average meeting does suffer from many of these dysfunctions, and, as a result, the quality of output is often suboptimal.

In 1939, Alex Osborne, an ad executive, was grappling with improving the quality of ideas. In a typical group setting when new ideas are being generated, various factors are at play, including group pressure, organizational politics, people's shyness to share a seemingly dumb idea, or uncertainty if the organization would have appetite for a radical idea. To counter these biases and prejudices, Alex created a "conference technique by which a group attempts to find a solution for a specific problem by amassing all the ideas spontaneously by its members," and called it "brainstorming."[5] He postulated following these four rules[6] to make an effective brainstorming session:

- **Focus on quantity.** The more ideas you produce, the greater your chances of hitting on something radical are.

- **Withhold criticism.** There are no bad ideas in a brainstorm.

- **Welcome unusual ideas.** Suspend your assumptions on the road to solutions.

- **Combine and improve ideas.** In other words, 1 + 1 = 3.

---

[5]Brainstorm means using the **brain** to **storm** a creative problem and to do so "in commando fashion, each stormer audaciously attacking the same objective.
[6]www.inc.com/the-build-network/the-real-don-draper-invented-brainstorming-but-he-did-it-wrong.html

By focusing on these five simple ground rules, he created a simple but highly effective system where participants didn't have to feel "threatened" to voice their ideas. Also, these rules "allowed" everyone to share their ideas, even if they were junior employees.

A basic brainstorming process works something like this:

1. Participants and facilitator identify/define the problem to be discussed. Quite often, we assume that everyone understands the problem equally, whereas, in reality, each person involved might have a very different understanding of what the problem is.

2. Participants write down everything that pops into their heads until they run out of ideas. This might be typically one of the following two flavors:

   a. an individual brainstorming session where everyone is given 10–15 minutes to write down their ideas before sharing with others.

   b. a group brainstorming session where participants might extend an idea or modify it, and so on.

3. Facilitator encourages creative flow of ideas by ensuring there is no bias, criticism, or premature evaluation of any idea until everyone has had a chance to present his or her ideas. This, in essence, is the divergent thinking part of the process—to be able to create as many options as the group can think of without prematurely determining which are useless or which are interesting but unusable. Many of the most successful ideas started their long and arduous journey as someone's silly idea. In fact, the main reason we want to brainstorm is to think of ideas outside of our comfort zone. So, at this stage of the process, we focus on capturing as many ideas as the group can generate.

4. Once all ideas have been presented, the facilitator coordinates collation by removing duplicates, clustering similar ideas, eliminating unfit ideas, and so on. We need to be careful here when we say "eliminating unfit ideas," since it is not often obvious which ideas are duds and which ones are potential goldmines? Hence, one might not want to rush into pruning the list lest some very promising ideas are thrown out.

5. The group discusses all ideas, selects promising ones, and prioritizes them for planning the next set of action items. While many teams tend to prioritize based on some kind of complexity or criticality to business, This is the convergent thinking part of the process. We have a large pool of ideas wherein we apply our collective brainpower to sift through them and understand which ones will likely be strong enough to go to the next stage. We also start synthesizing them to build upon the ideas.

For the next 50+ years, this largely remained as the single-most talked-about method (if not the most effective one!) to stoke creativity in business meetings. IDEO, the leading design firm, swears by it. However, due to improperly trained facilitators and unwilling participants, brainstorming got a bad name. Several studies have shown that, in fact, brainstorming is a more inferior technique than simply having people work independently on ideas and later pooling them.[7] There is also a fair bit of criticism that the quantity doesn't necessarily beget quality.

The original idea behind brainstorming was not bad—if anything, it was meant to free up creativity from the clutches of a select few (mostly the top leadership) and democratize the process so that everyone present in the room could participate.

However, over the years, it has lost its edge as an effective tool for generating ideas due to various factors, including inadequate preparation of participants, not having enough agreement or clarity about the goals of a session, ineffective or weak trainers, and politically driven agendas. Clearly, something more contemporary was needed.

Gamestorming

In knowledge work, we need our goals to be fuzzy.

—Gamestorming, Dave Gray et al.

Anyone who has been in a few brainstorming sessions will quickly notice that while they offer a relatively quick way to get a conversation started, the format of capturing and conveying information is mostly textual, and the meetings tend to be very dull and businesslike. Compare this to how human beings—mostly children, but even grownups—manage to have fun when playing games.

---

[7]www.newyorker.com/magazine/2012/01/30/groupthink?currentPage=all

Who says work can't be fun? Why can't a meeting be considered a "game" and the participants be considered "players" who are all playing by some common rules and are guided together by a shared goal?

If the team has a bit of fun doing things, it won't dilute the importance of a business meeting. In fact, if anything, it might stimulate more creative ideas and collaboration among the participants. Experience and research have shown that happy people are more creative and collaborative.[8]

This fact becomes even more profound when we consider that playing is a fundamental part of human nature. Unfortunately, the word "play" is often considered to be synonymous with "not working." Hence, it was generally looked down upon as a workplace practice for most of the industrial era. However, the advent of the knowledge era saw people using the gaming philosophy to stimulate creativity, breaking the monotony and injecting fun and energy into the rituals while fostering the spirit of teamwork and collaboration. In addition, it reduced the stress level of the participants.

With that perspective, the authors Sunni Brown, Dave Gray, and James Macanufo wrote an interesting book, *Gamestorming*. They attribute the genesis of gamestorming to Silicon Valley in the 1970s. They consider "game" a quick way to put a structure around a creative process to quickly organize a team into an ad-hoc way to collaborate and solve problems, especially the unknown-unknown or the complex ones. Much like the famous Brothers Grimm, they have essentially documented a lot of these "games" that have been around for several decades in the high-tech industry.

So, what is gamestorming? Let's first define what a game is.

A game can be deconstructed as a finite event that has boundaries in time and space with the spatial constraints of the game (for example, the swimming pool or a ping-pong table) where normal day-to-day rules of human interaction are replaced by a different set of mutually agreed-upon rules (for example, each of the pieces on a chessboard has different set of rules on how they could be moved). As long as the playtime is on (that is, within the temporal constraints of the game), these rules continue to govern this temporary, but real world. During this time, the players interact with each other using artifacts, like a football or an ice puck. And, finally, there is an end goal that tells when a game is over. In cricket, the team playing second must score the runs within the available time to be declared the winner.

---

[8] www.forbes.com/2010/08/13/happiest-occupations-workplace-productivity-how-to-get-a-promotion-morale-forbes-woman-careers-happiness.html

We all know this is not the real world, for every game has a finite life, and yet, the game has such power to bring its players together in pursuit of its collective goals. Sometimes there might be extrinsic rewards for accomplishing the objectives, but most often, teams come together because they believe in the cause and, hence, the rewards are mostly intrinsic in spirit.

Can we liken a business meeting to a game? If we can take a very broad view of what we try to accomplish in a meeting, it is a definitely possibility. And if we could do that, we could change the way people view meetings —rather than energy-sapping events, they regard them as fun and collaboration activities that leave them recharged and refreshed.

So, how would gamestorming be applied to an ideation session? Let's say you want to understand what are some of the pain points of your product or service. Traditionally, we might commission a user feedback survey, get the data, and brainstorm solutions. However, Luke Hohman suggested some ideas that might help solve problems such as these in a more creative and collaborative manner. In his 2007 book *Innovation Games*,[9] he suggests the game Speedboat where we take a speedboat as a visual metaphor of your product or service and anchors representing pain points that are slowing down the boat. This "same" information might be available in reams of documentation and customer feedback forms, but there is no comparison when you get your entire team working together in the room – including the customer—and build a visual speedboat collaboratively such that your team starts to see why exactly your customers feel that a particular issue is a pain point. When I conduct this activity, I can see the teams having fun and end up creating a very high-energy environment. Apart from the fun and collaborative environment, the output of the exercise is highly visual in nature, which stimulates higher engagement and invites action.

This is just one of over a dozen games that Luke captures in his book. Depending on your specific needs, he has given guidance on which is a more appropriate game. Luke's website has quite a lot of information on these games that can help you get started, but for a more in-depth and thorough understanding, I would recommend reading his book.

Bodystorming

Gamestorming raises the level of game to make it more collaborative and fun. It also exploits the power of visual thinking, which is certainly better received by the human brains. However, there might be problems that may still not be best captured or analyzed using gamestorming.

---

[9]http://innovationgames.com has good amount of information to get started on this topic.

Suppose you are exploring a very radical idea—something that the world hasn't quite seen, or at least you are personally not very familiar with it. For example, you want to build a new wheelchair that will make life much easier for people with temporary or extended immobility. Your team might consist of the best electrical engineers, mechanical engineers, software developers, and so on, but if none of you has ever experienced what it is like to sit in a wheelchair for longs periods of time, you might end up making a lot of technically correct functional decisions, but have no real idea about the users' needs. A gamestorming session might help build a higher level of empathy, but unless you have subjected yourself to near-real-life experience, it might not bring the finer aspects of what it takes to understand the small details vital to building a great solution. That's where bodystorming could help.

Simply put, bodystorming is all about using our human bodies to enact a given scenario and cull out important and finer aspects of a problem that otherwise might remain only broadly and superficially understood. In some situations, this could bring an altogether new level of thinking to problem solving.

Bodystorming is also a fun way to build first-hand empathy about limitations or situations that the team might not be able to fully grasp. For example, you are developing a new type of crutches that help improve people with disabilities' effectiveness. Unless you have been disabled, it might be extremely difficult to think of underlying use cases that might only be discovered when one has "lived" that life.

The Beta Cup[10] project was started in May 2009 because some people were concerned that 58 billion paper cups were sold each year—but never recycled. They employed bodystorming[11] to understand how they could conceive of a new product that could not only solve the problem but also make it fun and easy to use.

How do you do bodystorming? Well, there are no real rules. The only thing one really needs to do is to get off the chair[12] and involve their human bodies in enacting the product or the service they wish to get more insights about.

Depending on the kind of problem you are solving, bodystorming might be a great alternative way to develop deeper insights about the problem being solved. It might offer better ROI than simply sitting in a meeting room and brainstorming what "might" be the real-world issues, or even collaborating with the customer during a gamestorming session.

---

[10]http://thebetacup.com/
[11]https://vimeo.com/5968946
[12]https://dschool.stanford.edu/groups/k12/wiki/48c54/Bodystorming.html

Trystorming

Sometimes we end up spending far too much time and effort in simply thinking and talking about things when "doing" might help us understand the problems much better. For example, instead of brainstorming about a mobile app that helps finds your lost dog, why not simply build a prototype and see what happens?

Today's technology and tools make it extremely easy to build software in a very rapid manner. If you are offering your products or services over the Internet (and who isn't nowadays?), you can quickly find a way to deliver to a test group across the Web and get feedback from real humans (a term used to make developers remember that their opinions are only a second-best guess and that the feedback that counts comes from real users, not from friends or family).

So, what is trystorming? Put simply, it is using the hands to "build" a rapid prototype instead of making PowerPoint slides or Word documents about it. The prototype doesn't need to be perfect or have polished edges. In fact, its utility stems from the least amount of time and effort it requires to put something up on the table that could start conversations. Clearly, the more refined such a prototype is, the more resistance to feedback or criticism one could expect from its creator. Hence, it is often better to build something that demonstrate, or helps validate, the key aspects of the problem or the riskiest assumptions behind it.

In their book *Toyota by Toyota*, authors Samuel Obara and Darril Wilburn describe trystorming as "the hands-on version of brainstorming," and provide a context to trystorming as the following:

> ... Trystorming is the antidote when team members are already exhausted from meticulous and thorough brainstorming and they are borderline becoming too comfortable in their chairs. I think there is some truth to the adage "analysis paralysis," in that after some time sitting, thinking, and talking, we become paralyzed by the inertia and our bodies are numbed up like zombies at the end of a long movie.

There are some interesting articles that describe how trystorming could be utilized[13] and that describe how Japanese companies put it in practice.[14]

---

[13]www.thefreelibrary.com/Establishing+a+Kaizen+culture%3a+on+%22trystorming%2c%22+and+why+%22best%22+is...-a0171685315

[14]http://pebblestorm.com/2008/06/24/better-than-brainstorming-trystorming/

All said, I am a big believer of trystorming as a means to develop deeper understanding about the problem and to get the conversations between the customer and the development flowing. This is especially beneficial in our industry where writing a few lines of code to quickly test out an idea or a hypothesis is perhaps the least time- or effort-consuming of them all.

Hackathons

Popularized by high-tech companies from Silicon Valley, hackathon culture has gradually permeated across the globe, at least in the high-tech industry. It is a great way to align energies and resources of entire organization and focus them to solve an important problem—all while having fun.

In its simplest form, a hackathon is all about creating a special fun-filled atmosphere for 24 to 48 hours where a group of people form teams and build a quick hack to solve some problem innovatively. The idea is not to create PowerPoint-laden business plans, but rather working software that helps demonstrate the happy path of a use case. The spirit of the event and its carnival-style atmosphere helps lower the anxiety levels related to risk of failure among participants. However, in a hackathon, we want participants to completely change their thinking and do something totally crazy, something that they might never do unless someone guarantees them total immunity from ridicule, reprisal, and rejection (never mind that quite often, we may not even get any real idea worth next year's business plan).

Why will we want to put organizational time, effort, and money into something like this? After all, we might not get any ROI on this!

Hackathons help address some of the major impediments to an innovation culture by doing the following:

- Empowering people. Innovation is democratized, and just about anyone can bring in new ideas. If the idea is any good, rest assured, it can quickly find favor among the upper management.

- Eliminating fear or embarrassment of failure. When we are not being judged by the quality of our efforts, it is easy to think completely wildly, and sometimes that can propel the creative thinking in ways like never before.

- Creating fun. When people are having fun, it takes away the pressure to perform. While it might appear to the uninitiated that people are slacking off and not really being "productive," I consider this as the organization-wide teambuilding experience that eventually pays off by creating a culture of collaborative problem solving in a fun-filled manner.

- Providing help. In any reasonable product, there are several moving parts, and it is literally impossible for any single engineer to come up with a complete solution. A hackathon, thus, helps provide a platform where the success depends on a small group of engineers with cross-functions skills coming together and producing working software in a small amount of time.

- Thinking bite size. Unless there are constraints that limit the time (and resources) available to solve the problem, it is unlikely that the team will zero in on the crux of the problem.

- Encouraging speed. By limiting the time to 24 or 48 hours, the team is under pressure to deliver the goods fast. This also allows the team to identify newer ways to quickly solve problems.

- Lowering the barriers to innovation. Sometimes we unnecessarily bloat the entire decision-making or execution process and end up doing no real work. By contrast, a hackathon is completely bereft of the administrative red tape, making it far easier for innovation to happen.

I consider a hackathon to be like a mass-scale trystorming. It is a very small investment of an organization's time, effort, and money, and when done under the right conditions, it can spur up an organization's culture by encouraging people to take meaningful risks and develop ideas that hold potential.

Medici Effect

A hackathon is often a diverse group of professionals who all decide to come together for a finite period of time and collaborate on a common problem. What if such a confluence were not confined by short time limits, but were allowed to happen in a more systemic manner and for a longer time period? What would happen if people stepped outside their comfort zones and agreed to work together at the intersection of their respective competencies without ever worrying about the pressure of delivering some pre-determined output?

Frans Johansson's 2006 book *The Medici Effect: What Elephants and Epidemics Can Teach Us About Innovation* is a great read. Based on the fifteenth-century banking family in Florence that funded a multitude of innovations, Johansson presents a compelling argument that "when you step into an intersection of fields, disciplines or cultures, you can combine existing concepts into a large number of extraordinary new ideas." He calls it the *Medici Effect*.

Johansson's fascinating body of research shows that when you purposefully bring people from diverse skill sets together and allow to them intermingle without any specific agenda, the result is invariably something of great value. He calls such an intersection as "your best chance to innovate."

Creating the Medici Effect might require much more time and careful efforts than some of the methods discussed earlier, but it is certainly much more powerful and sustaining. It might enable an organization to build upon a culture of sharing and learning that fosters teamwork and collaboration, and gradually builds a DNA of innovation.

Conclusion

When embarking on innovation, a classic conundrum is whether to pursue an idea until you eventually find a way to turn it into a product and solve a real-world problem, or to take up current pain points and solve them?

I once attended a talk by Scott Cook, Founder of Intuit, who outlined Intuit's innovation strategy—find the pain points and solve them. Simple. While this approach to innovation might reflect a highly customer-driven mindset and could be very effective, it might have limitations in terms of creating radical or disruptive innovative ideas. As an example, Intuit was not able to extend its leadership in the online space and, while it had Quickenonline as an internal program, it finally had to shell out $170 million to buy mint.com to augment its online offering.[15]

So, what is the best way forward for companies looking for the next big idea? Clearly, there is no one right answer. In fact, depending on one's unique context, more than one approach might be needed to triangulate the right set of ideas to pursue.

In this chapter, we have discussed some of the techniques that can help quickly identify probable sets of ideas that could be taken up in the value chain for further deliberation. We have not included all the techniques (for example, we have not talked about Chindogu, Jugaad, or the McGuyver-style of innovation), and some of the techniques such as Design Thinking and Lean Startups will be discussed later in this book. We hope that the chapter has given you a quick overview of the underlying ideas behind ideation techniques.

---

[15]http://voices.washingtonpost.com/fasterforward/2010/07/intuit_quashes_quicken_online.html

Peter Thiel's latest book, *Zero to One*, offers an interesting metaphor with an undeniable patter. Going from "zero to one" creates a unique value that invariably comes from a disruptor (think of Yahoo, Google, Facebook, Twitter, LinkedIn, and Snapchat at the time they were created) but over time, each one had to scale horizontally. Most of them had to rely on shopping other disruptors who were busy crafting their own "zero to one" journey (Whatsapp, Instagram, Broadcast.com, Android, and so on) to keep their innovation engine running. At last count, Google had done 178 acquisitions,[16] Yahoo! had done 112 acquisitions,[17] Cisco had done 170 acquisitions,[18] and even a company as young as Facebook had done 53 acquisitions.[19]

So, who would you rather be—the company that acquires innovation or the one who actually creates it?

---

[16]https://en.wikipedia.org/wiki/List_of_mergers_and_acquisitions_by_Google
[17]https://en.wikipedia.org/wiki/List_of_mergers_and_acquisitions_by_Yahoo!
[18]https://en.wikipedia.org/wiki/List_of_acquisitions_by_Cisco_Systems
[19]https://en.wikipedia.org/wiki/List_of_mergers_and_acquisitions_by_Facebook

Deliberate

To do or not to do?

New ideas pass through three periods: (1) It can't be done. (2) It probably can be done, but it's not worth doing. (3) I knew it was a good idea all along!

—*Arthur C. Clarke*

Eureka!

You think you have found an idea that can change the world ...

Great!

Now, what next?

This question befuddles many product managers and entrepreneurs alike. How should we decide if the cool new technical idea is really a great product idea worth pursuing? Should we conduct market research first and gauge the market opportunity, or should we simply go out and build the product before a competitor gets a whiff of it? How do we convince the upper management to fund this great idea? Or, should we try to build something on the side (like a Skunk Works)? Should we fortify our first-mover advantage by protecting some of the intellectual property, or open source it to make it more likely to be adopted by the wider community? How do we know if people really want this idea? How soon can we get this feedback so that we could build a better product or cut our losses sooner rather than later? These questions, among others, make the journey of product development interesting, challenging, and rewarding. Of course, there are no quick or ready-made answers, and the answers that worked the last time might not apply here—hence, you must start the journey afresh every time.

Stealth Mode Development

The most common approach to product development involves taking the most promising ideas (often based on intuition) and developing them into products in a "stealth mode." In a stealth mode, companies typically cut themselves off from mainstream civilization and choose to complete a product built primarily on their assessment of what the problem is and what the solution should be instead of getting any early feedback or validation from the customers. Companies hypothesize that they understand enough about the problem their customers are facing to know the right solution to build. Hence, they don't consider slowing down the process by introducing any feedback loops in between steps. Being an early mover is clearly one of the goals, and fear of competition makes companies wary of sharing their idea prematurely, even for the purpose of obtaining potentially life-saving feedback.

During the infamous dotcom meltdown, dozens of companies folded because they chose to build products without fully deliberating upon what the right product ideas worth pursuing were. They chose to build out every single conceivable product feature without determining if there was a market for it or not. The result was that while they built a fully scaled, fancy-looking product or service, they unfortunately didn't have a large enough customer base to make the product launch as interesting and successful as the product development journey had been. During the time that briefly preceded the NASDAQ crash in March 2000 and some two years after that, over 800 Internet companies collapsed.[1] Some notable examples include Webvan.com, ePets.com, and Toys.com. Most of these companies had unrealistic valuations without any regard to a proven and repeatable business model.

Despite the recent history of obvious pitfalls of such an approach, we still find takers for this grand way of building products. This method requires a long runway (meaning, a long supply of funding and patience), but more importantly, the belief that we the makers know better than the consumers. In a way, this is like Henry Ford saying, "Had we gone to the people, they would have told us faster horses."—a sentiment doesn't quite apply in today's world. Clearly, the current thinking is not about making products in isolation or with an arrogance that we know better than our customers.

In today's ever-changing world, a successful approach asks these three fundamental questions:

- What is the problem?
- Who are the customers?
- What do they want?

---

[1] www.businessplanarchive.org/whatwecanlearn/statsummary.php

What is the problem?

Very often, the entrepreneurs are strong techies who have a great understanding of the solution domain, such as how to build the next cool search engine or design a great web site. However, they don't always know or fully understand why anyone would want their cool product. In fact, I have seen a clear pattern—the stronger the techies are, the more likely they have their own view of what the problem is without much perspective from the potential customers. The result is often a great fancy toy that looks cool to play with, but whether it solves a customer problem or not is often a big question mark.

Who are my customers?

When you are a bunch of techies building an elegant solution without really exposing it to "real humans," chances are you will end up building one that only similarly qualified techies (or unqualified users, depending on how you look at it) can use. Knowing who your potential customers are is not only needed to elicit the right set of requirements, but it is also a great mechanism to validate the fundamental hypotheses around the intended solution. The typical advice for entrepreneurs is to go beyond "friends and family" and talk to "real humans" to discover your customers.

What do they want?

Finding out what customers want is the key to product development. In the past, as Eddie Obeng puts it so well,[2] our rate of learning surpassed the pace of change around us. However, today these two lines have crossed and the pace of change not only surpasses our ability to learn, but the gap is also increasing. In such a world, there is no way we can make fixed assumptions about what people want from a given product or service. Instead, we need to constantly explore what interests them. As Steve Blank puts it so firmly, the only real way to discover what your customer wants is to "get out of the building" and talk to real humans—that's where the facts exist. Inside a meeting room, we only have opinions.

Well, who ever said product development was easy?

Collaborative Development

Given the previous argument, it seems fairly logical that a far better way to develop products is by having continuous interaction between the creators and the consumers.

---

[2]https://youtu.be/yVIe1MOpiHU

In the last several years, new product development has clearly and irreversibly tilted to a more collaborative approach. New product development is often co-created rather than built on the shaky foundations of mass production thinking.

In the rest of this chapter, we will explore some of these contemporary approaches and discuss the techniques for evaluating ideas before we start to build better products.

Prototyping

Prototyping can be best understood by applying economics of software development.

When people think of a "prototype," they often imagine a scaled-down version of the actual object that moves and behaves pretty much the same way as the real thing. While there is some truth to this concept of a prototype, it makes assumptions about what goes into building a prototype. For example, if you spend huge amounts of time, effort, and money to build a prototype, chances are that it might be too late and too costly to build the actual product. And, most importantly, it may not be amenable to making changes (imagine being told that after spending half a million dollars, your prototype needs some serious revisions!).

The current thinking is all about building prototypes commensurate with the context of business and the phase one is in. As we will discuss in the rest of this section, even a napkin is a great tool to "prototype" an idea when you don't have anything concrete yet, but you do want to communicate your ideas to interested stakeholders or potential customers. However, much later in the product life cycle, the same napkin might not be the most effective tool anymore.

In the context of software development, the current trend is to minimize the amount of software written and to maximize the amount of learning we can glean from putting the prototype in customers' hands. After all, the customers neither know what programming language was used nor care how much code was written to make the prototype happen. But minimizing written software means actively seeking other tools that allow a product to be created, often with a minimum or no amount of software being written. Reducing the amount of software not only reduces the time and effort to build a prototype, but it also makes it relatively "easy" for a criticism to be accepted by its creator.

A good prototype should be easy to discard after it has served its purpose. This is where the economics of software development makes even more sense. When we realize that the prototype is only an experiment whose real purpose is to generate feedback and not ship software code, we are in a better position to embrace the idea of minimizing the amount of time, effort, and money invested upfront in creating it.

Prototypes are typically classified as either low-fidelity or high-fidelity. As their names suggest, a low-fidelity prototype is rather abstract and incomplete in terms of details as opposed to a high-fidelity prototype that has richer and deeper details. A low-fidelity prototype allows a broad-level inspection of the key assumptions about a future product's intended user interface, whereas a high-fidelity prototype is much more closer to the final end-product. A low-fidelity prototype is of great value in the initial stages of product development because it encourages conversation around key design principles and assumptions about the product. On the other hand, a high-fidelity prototype is much more useful in the later stages of the product and allows for more fine-grained feedback about how to make the product more useful.

In this book, we have restricted our discussion to low-level design because it is more contextual to building products using agile thinking. To that end, we have limited our discussion to methods and techniques that don't require anything more than a pen and a paper. We recognize that as the ideas mature, the team will need to evolve toward high-fidelity prototypes and will also require specialists in user experience, graphic design, interaction design, and user interface design.

Back of Napkin

What is the fastest and most effective way you can communicate your idea to a peer, a collaborator, a leader, an investor, or a customer? We often write reams of documentation or present tons of slides to share our ideas, or we simply start building them as a full-fledged product. While writing about an idea might be relatively fast and cheap, it might not convey the entire picture. Building the product prematurely might be time-consuming and costly. So, what if there were some very simple "template" to sketch out the most important elements of an idea during its initial phase—something that will capture the essence without taking a lot of time?

In 1986, Bill Zeidman designed the "Silicon Valley Napkin" so that "a prospective entrepreneur need only complete the check boxes in order to have a business plan ready to present to a venture capitalist for funding."

Here's how he explains what he did[3]:

> "In 1986 I created the Silicon Valley Napkin and began marketing and selling it. The printer required minimum print runs in the thousands, so I had boxes stacked to the ceiling in the kitchen of my one-bedroom apartment. By 1990, the napkin had run its course, and

---

[3]http://www.siliconvalleynapkin.com/

I still had boxes left. I approached The Garage, the precursor to the Tech Museum, to make a napkin donation. They were excited to have the napkins at their invitation-only, kickoff donor event, and I was glad to supply them."

It only takes a small amount of real estate to put across your idea (and, conversely, your idea is probably way too complex if you can't fit it on something like the Silicon Valley Napkin).

The napkins sound like a cool idea, but are they actually useful? Perhaps the most famous of them all is Southwest's story. In 1967, Rollin King and Herb Kelleher famously drew their idea on a cocktail napkin that eventually became Southwest Airlines. (See Figure 3-1 for my attempt to re-draw their original idea on a cocktail napkin.)

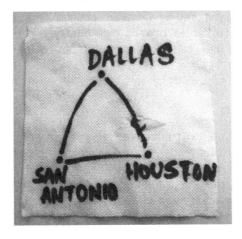

Figure 3-1. The idea behind Southwest Airlines was initially drawn on a cocktail napkin

King and Kelleher were leaving a failed airline, and they wanted to start a new airline with just three destinations. They found themselves in a pub, where the only thing available paper to doodle their idea on was a cocktail napkin. In fact, they value their napkin experience so much that they now print their route maps on napkins.

More recently, in 2008, Dan Roam wrote *The Back of a Napkin*. Roam believes that any problem can be made clearer with a picture, and any picture can be made using a simple set of tools and rules. He uses the humble "paper napkin" as a possible tool for quickly communicating ideas on a tangible medium, claiming that the napkin is a more powerful tool than Excel or PowerPoint. Roam claims that if you can draw basic geometric figures such as straight lines, arrows, circles, squares, and triangles, you are "guaranteed to become a better visual thinker." We are not talking about making someone a world-class graphic artist but rather using visual elements to enhance the thinking process.

Visual thinking is extremely effective in engaging a group of people who are trying to solve a complex problem. Representing the idea pictorially helps illustrate the connections between the different aspects in a manner that simply can't be accomplished in written text.

Paper Prototyping

A napkin is a great starting point. However, assuming that someone buys into your idea and provides you with the funding to get started, you don't immediately go out and build them the full product! In fact, prototyping is a continuous journey of learning. A good product developer engages different prototyping tools and techniques through the product creation process to get different types of feedback at different points in time.

Carolyn Snyder is a user experience consultant who specializes in qualitative user research and usability testing. In her 2003 book, *Paper Prototyping: The Fast and Easy Way to Design and Refine User Interfaces* explains how something as simple as using paper to create a low-fidelity prototype can be a very effective means for creating rapid feedback. She defines it in the following way:

> Paper prototyping is a variation of usability testing where representative users perform realistic tasks by interacting with a paper version of the interface that is manipulated by a person "playing computer," who doesn't want to explain how the interface is intended to work.

Without writing a single piece of software code, a developer (ideally it might make sense to have a design engineer on the team, but if you don't have one, it's not a bad idea for the developers to start the conversation rather than wait for an expert to arrive) can initiate a conversation with a prospective customer or an end-user. In just a matter of hours, the developer can determine what the customer might be looking for in a product.

Figure 3-2 illustrates a very rudimentary paper prototype for "bill pay" functionality as one of the features. It took me less than a few minutes to draw, but it allows me to show it to my customer and get her feedback if this is what she had in mind. She might come back with feedback that she doesn't want to offer the "pay later" option and just wants to keep it simple for now. Instead of making all the efforts to implement it and then discover her preference, my paper prototype has created the opportunity to learn of that preference before I even get started. Also, my customer wouldn't have been able to get such a clear picture of what I had in mind if not for such a visual representation of the user interface.

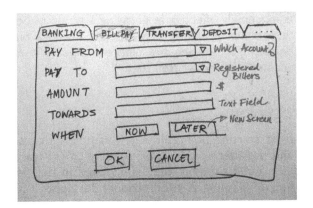

Figure 3-2. A paper prototype could be a crude drawing of the user interface

The prototype might begin with a blank sheet of paper that the developer gradually fills in with various elements of the user interface, without much regard to its relative positioning or sizing. At this point, the developer is only trying to get a visual dump of the mental models around the user interface for an intended product.

However, I prefer doing something a bit more "rearrangable" by using Post-it notes. Let's say I want to build a travel site and offer services for people to book flight tickets, hotels, holidays, and so on. Technically there is nothing new in any of these ideas anymore—pretty much anyone can offer these services in literally no time. The secret is to find out which are key requirements from the customer's point of view, and how best a layout would appeal to them. I could draw something like Figure 3-3 to show how a paper prototype could be created using Post-it notes.

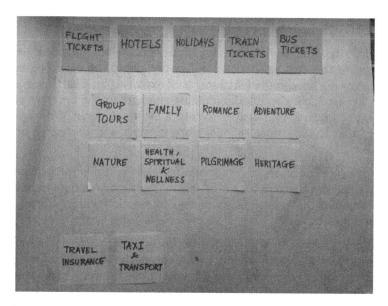

Figure 3-3. A paper prototype using Post-it notes

These Post-it notes could be created by crowdsourcing from inside the team and with the customers, and a working session could help establish a visual layout.

Using Post-it notes (or even simple colored paper notes, which is what I used for this particular picture) makes it a lot easier to make changes based on the conversation and feedback that a paper drawing might inhibit. When the goal of the activity is to get creative juices flowing in order to better understand and validate customer needs, it only makes sense to work on a medium that doesn't convey a sense of "finality," especially in the initial stages of the exploration.

Once I have something like this, I can present it to my target customers and get their feedback. For example, it turns out that my target customers care more for adventure and nature; I might want to prominently position these options and even decide to remove the other options from my main page lest I encourage a feeling among my target customers that I am not a specialized "vertical" site but a very generic "horizontal" one and, hence, might lack the real experience that they might be looking for.

Based on a series of interactions, we might lock down the high-level screen layout and get ready to understand how an old-school 2D engineering drawing of the product's user interface would look. Or, more simply, let's just call it a wireframe.

Wireframes

A paper prototype is often a crude way to express the key functionalities without any regard to visual aesthetics, usability, or operational ease. Nonetheless, it serves a key purpose in the initial stages of exploring an idea. However, once we have a reasonably good understanding and agreement on what customers are expecting, we will need to go into a bit more detail. We might need something that is a bit more refined, more tangible, and, perhaps, a bit more actionable.

A wireframe improves on its predecessors (that is, paper prototypes or a napkin doodle) by creating a two-dimensional, spatially proportioned visual representation of the key elements of user interaction with the product's or the object's interfaces.

Let's say I am trying to build a page for displaying user profiles for a social networking platform that I am building. I want to see the headshot of the person, some recent pictures that they have shared, and maybe some text about them that includes their interests, their hobbies, what kind of people they like to hang out with, and so on. I could try to explain this in a document, or I could try to communicate verbally—one will require a significant amount of time and effort in writing it, while the other could take reasonable efforts to draw a "pie in the sky," but still not establish a common medium on which I could easily collaborate with my customer. Or I could just spend a few minutes and create something like Figure 3-4 with any of the freely available products on the web to communicate what I have in mind.

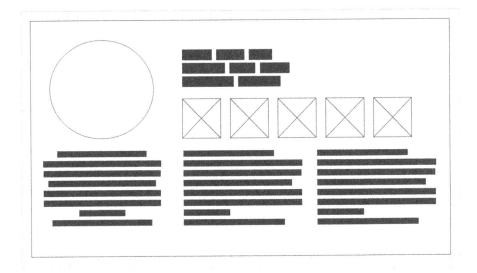

Figure 3-4. A wireframe offers a more realistic and proportionate depiction of the layout

I could share it with my target customers and ask them to give feedback, or I could share several variants of the layout and ask them to tell me which one they like (or even identify elements of each one that they like so I could mash them up into a single new one). Or, I could always sit down with them and let them co-create it. In all these situations, I can expect to get a much higher level of feedback in a comparatively short amount of time.

Even though the wireframe is totally devoid of any fancy-looking colors or high-resolution graphics, it captures the essence of the product as far as user interaction is concerned by depicting key elements of the user interface, their relative positioning on the interface, and their intended behaviors. It is a gradual and progressive refinement of the idea as it gets transformed into a full-fledged product. At this point, it is still not anywhere close to being a working prototype, but might suffice in terms of its look and feel, and, in the hands of a potential user, it gives an opportunity for early feedback on key assumptions and decisions.

Mock-ups

A mock-up picks up where a wireframe stops. It includes more details in the user interface than a wireframe and facilitates further discussion about the emotional connect of the product with its intended users. It can offer richer details about the intended product so that users can see how the final product might look like. They can decide if they would like to make any major changes before the same look and feel is replicated in the final product.

Creating a mock-up might require writing software code, though, increasingly, it doesn't have to. Tools such as Keynotopia offer a smart way to convert a PowerPoint or a keynote presentation into a mock-up in less than 30 minutes by creating a series of highly interactive mock-up screens. These screens give a more dynamic representation of the workflow.

Let's say I am building a new web site called MyDreamHome that allows a property owner to sell and/or lease and an interested buyer to buy and/or rent properties. I am trying various options for the initial screen layout, and I want to know if my prospective users will like some visual layout aspects over others. I could use any of the several available software to quickly create a layout like the one in Figure 3-5 and, instead of asking them over a phone call or an e-mail, give them something tangible to think about in order to make a choice. In this case, making a mock-up like this costs me less than ten minutes and, though it is a static prototype (meaning, none of the buttons are clickable), it still offers a starting point for the conversation.

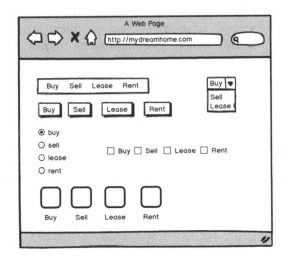

Figure 3-5. With modern-day tools, realistic-looking mock-ups can be created very quickly

Note that a mock-up might still not offer the intended functionality—if it does, it tends to be more like a prototype, though it doesn't have to. What is important is that it allows the conversations between the creator and the consumer to proceed to the next level where more specific decisions can be made about delivering the desired functionality in the most effective manner. The true payoff of a mock-up is that we get a disproportionately large amount of feedback by putting in relatively small amounts of time and effort in building it. Surely, if the mock-up is extremely bad, you might get a lot of feedback, but it might shake a customer's confidence in your ability to understand the problem and design a solution. On the other hand, a completely detailed, pixel-perfect mock-up might not only take too much time and effort to be effective in terms of a real ROI, it might also put off prospective users into thinking that the product is already done. A designer or a developer must keep these finer points in mind while exploring the options to get to the right level of details.

Design Thinking

In the previous section, we discussed prototyping as the means to expedite feedback before the team starts detailing out the product. The key principles behind prototyping are, once again, economics—how can we ensure that we are able to validate our key assumptions before incurring irrecoverable time, effort, and money, sometimes referred to as the "sunk costs." However, prototyping only offers the operational tools and techniques to systematically and progressively evolve a product's design.

A lot of traditional product developers, especially in the software industry, often establish the technology and architecture first, and then try to retrofit the user experience and the user interface into what the technology allows. Many of us are building products with a technical mindset that is not appropriate for the average user. This realization enraged Alan Cooper, and he ended up writing the classic 1998 book *The Inmates Are Running the Asylum*, in which he argues that we techies are basically unqualified to write software and build systems for the technically illiterate human beings. Having been a software developer myself, I can very well relate to it. In several cases, we techies used to design the user experience for totally non-technical users, such as nurses or normal people who watch television, and the results left much to be desired! So how do we make sure we don't build technologically superior products that don't serve any real useful value for its target users?

In the last few years, the term "design thinking" has taken off as one of the most fancied buzzwords. Even though most people don't really understand what it means, much less what it can do for them, there is an active interest in learning more about it.

Tim Brown of IDEO defines "design thinking" in the following way:

> Design thinking is a human-centered approach to innovation that draws from the designer's toolkit to integrate the needs of people, the possibilities of technology, and the requirements for business success.

Tom Kelly in *Change by Design* describes design thinking's mission as follows:

> The mission of design thinking is to translate observation into insights, and insights into products and services that will improve lives.

Design thinking is the process that combines the elements of people (desirability), business (viability), and technology (feasibility) and seeks to build products that solve real needs of people.

Figure 3-6 illustrates IDEO's philosophy behind design thinking.

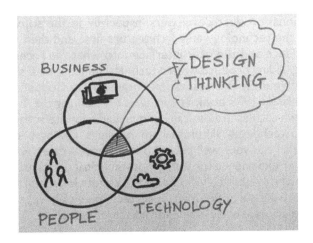

Figure 3-6. Design thinking is at the center of interaction among people, technology, and business

Design thinking is both a process and a mindset. Stanford's Design School has identified seven key mindsets[4] that facilitate a design thinker:

1. **Focus on human values:** Design thinking is first and foremost about empathy for the people for whom we are designing solutions. In the absence of a genuine empathy, we tend to make ignorant assumptions or become judgmental and end up designing products that conform to our mental models rather than acknowledging the real pain felt by the people who go through the problem every day.

2. **Show, don't tell:** Instead of talking about something, we want people to build something that allows them to present their vision and ideas visually and with more compelling storytelling, or by creating impactful and meaning experiences. I often go to the point where you learn more by simply showing something and there is no tell at all—let the people "give" you feedback based on how they interact with the object.

---

[4] http://dschool.stanford.edu/wp-content/uploads/2011/03/BootcampBootleg2010v2SLIM.pdf

3. **Embrace experimentation:** I consider experimentation as the unit of progress, especially when solving complex problems that haven't been solved before. We must start with a beginner's mindset and not be afraid to ask questions and conduct small experiments that help us validate our assumptions and put us on a learning path. Of course, mistakes will be made and some amount of time and effort will have to be discarded while pursuing the path of experimentation. However, without experimentation, we might be doomed to accept even bigger costs should our strategy, largely unvalidated, happen to be nothing more than a mirage.

4. **Be mindful of process:** Even as we say that a design thinker must have the right mindset to be effective in solving problems and designing better solutions and that the whole process is not really a predictable process in the traditional sense, there is still a close-ended orientation to the entire activity. At the end of the day, this is not a science project or something that is only being pursued for someone's happiness alone! We are committed to solving real-world problems and, hence, there must be a sense of how well are we progressing, how we are keeping the stakeholders involved and communicated, and, if there is an overall "process" that we have agreed to follow, how we are doing on it.

5. **Bias towards action:** Let the word "thinking" in design thinking not mislead you, for design thinking is more about "doing" than thinking. Having ideas is a great thing, but if we fail to translate them into something tangible that others can see, touch, and feel, we might not be able to get any meaningful feedback that helps us validate our raw assumptions and make tangible progress. As a design thinker, we are more like "thinking with hands" than a usual thinking with the mind alone.

6. **Radical collaboration:** Any non-trivial problems have so many moving parts that it is virtually impossible for any one individual to understand them all equally well. Designing a great solution might require an understanding of the underlying technology, the markets, product landscape, fundamental human behavior, pricing, cost of manufacturing, materials technology, supply chains, marketing and distribution channels, and so on. When teams are small and close-knit, they rely upon each other to find the best solutions rather than apportioning responsibility (and often blame) on each other.

7. **Craft clarity:** Our solution, or prototype, will reflect our clarity about a given problem. If a solution hasn't been well crafted, it will fail to inspire the prospective users to consider it, and we will lose the opportunity to get meaningful feedback on it. The most successful products of our generation are not the ones that make its user think, but hide the technical complexity under the product's surface and craft the level of clarity that is aligned to the user's mindset rather than the developer's mindset.

These mindsets are a great learning tool for anyone aspiring to become an effective design thinker (and, yes, anyone can become a better and effective design thinker with enough learning and practice).

In addition to being a mindset, design thinking is also a process, but not in the traditional sense of a series of fixed steps with a rigid sequence. Any design thinking process typically starts with developing a deep empathy about the target users, followed by a divergent effort to explore as many solutions as possible. The next step is to prune down this list of solutions by choosing the most promising ideas that go on to be prototyped and refined iteratively with user feedback. Different schools and organizations have developed their own version of the design thinking process, but the essence remains similar to this. Instead of looking for one sight solution, we are willing to explore multiple options that help us understand various facets of the problem better. By not prematurely converging onto a solution, we allow ourselves to think of better alternatives than simply copying the solution that worked the last time. Finally, the whole loop of prototyping, iterating, and receiving feedback allows us to get invaluable insight on patterns that might work better. We are not looking for one single prototype to be the eventual winner, but we are often looking for individual patterns to be discovered through these short-cycle experiments that allow us to build some kind of a repository of successful patterns. Once we have found what works and have tested it rigorously enough, we are on the way to solving the problem.

Figure 3-7 illustrates IDEO's design thinking process looks. While the process seems to be a linear flow from left to right, it is only to reflect the key activities undertaken, which could flow in any direction depending on the ground realities. However, a complete run of the design thinking process will typically involve all these key steps and will roughly flow in this fashion, though internal flows among various steps are perfectly normal.

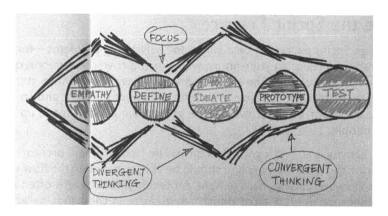

Figure 3-7. A design thinking process is not a single-pass sequence of steps

While a design thinking process is often visually represented to look like a linear process, in reality it is anything but a linear sequential process! While each of the atomic elements do constitute a specific functional aspect of the overall process, the interaction and the flows inside a design thinking process are highly fluid, and are more driven by the way a given problem unfolds itself rather than a pre-determined and fixed sequence of steps. To that end, it is once again a mindset even when operating within the context of a "process."

To recap, design thinking as an approach to solve problems emphasizes the following key elements:

- Empathy—not just functional / technological solutions

- Creativity—not just known / obvious solutions

- Learning—iterating through prototypes leads to feedback

Google Ventures has created a very specific adaptation of design thinking that they call "Design Sprints." Design Sprints is a five-day structured process for solving problems in a very structured manner using the principles of design thinking.

Google Ventures' Design Sprints

Google Ventures design partner Jake Knapp developed the design thinking process from IDEO and Stanford's Design School into a structured and optimized process known as Design Sprint.[5] It takes a product or a feature from design through prototyping and testing within a week. He has run over 100 sprints within Google and with startups within Google Ventures' portfolio.

Here's how the process goes:

---

[5]The Design Sprint, http://www.gv.com/sprint/

Before the Sprint: Prepare

The Design Sprint process is best suited for solving big problems—for example, you want to redesign your entire web site, improve conversions, or solve another critical problem. The process involves having the entire startup or the product team—CEO, designer, architect, product manager, and so on—in the same room for the next five days. A good team is often made up of four to eight people.

One key activity is to find a good facilitator. The facilitator will orchestrate the activities for the next five days and should be able to maintain the flow of ideas while being aware of time management. An external facilitator is often recommended because the facilitator doesn't participate in the hands-on activities, but rather runs the process as effectively as possible.

Enlisting users for the prototype testing at the end of the sprint should be done as soon as possible. Several startups within Google Ventures' portfolio are known to use simple methods such as advertising for (paid) users on Craigslist. Doing so at this stage ensures that all the users are available for the fifth day of the Design Sprint.

Other steps in preparation involve taking care of the logistics, such as scheduling the event and procuring resources (basic office supplies such as tape, white sheets, sticky notes, sharpies, and timers as well as a large conference room).

Day 1: Understand

The focus of the first day of the sprint is understanding the problem as deeply and comprehensively as possible. Having all key stakeholders in the room ensures that the team is able to build individual understandings into a common understanding of the problem to be solved.

The team could utilize a number of techniques to broaden its common understanding. For example, the CEO could present on the business opportunity, while a product manager could demo a competitor's product or share analytics. The designer could share ideas about improving user experience, while techies could explain some tech stacks that might help improve system performance. A time limit of each of these presentations of ten minutes is recommended to keep the conversation flowing while covering as many aspects of the problem as possible.

Once the group has had the opportunity to share various perspectives, the team can start evolving its understanding of the single most important "user story" for the current sprint. In my experience, this should be the most important value your product or service aims to offer, or the biggest pain point that threatens to wipe out your customer base. This user story should be expressed as visually as possible.

For any non-trivial problem, it's perfectly possible that this user story is too large to be prototyped within a short sprint of five days. In such cases, the team needs to refine part of the user story into areas that should be subjected to the user story on Day 5. In other words, what would you as a team like to know better that will help you make more-informed decisions in the following weeks?

At the end of Day 1, the team has chosen some important ideas that they would like to learn about in the next few days.

Day 2: Diverge

The team begins Day 2 at the point where it ended Day 1—at a common understanding of the problem and what aspect of the problem it would like to solve during the current sprint. On Day 2, the team works toward exploring as many solutions as possible. The team exploits divergent thinking. As opposed to traditional brainstorming, which has its known perils, the team works individually and often silently—without worrying about how will their ideas will get implemented, or if they even make sense.

One way the team accomplishes such ideation at speed is by using perhaps the lowest-fidelity prototypes—paper prototypes. There is no need to be pixel-perfect at this time. Rather, by focusing on a very high-level "appearance" of a user interface, the team can focus on the most important elements instead of embellishing the idea prematurely. For example, one of the techniques described is "Crazy Eights" where each team member comes up with eight sketches of an idea within five minutes. If there are eight people in the room, you have sixty-four possible user-interface sketches within five minutes. That's a lot of input for the next stage, which is storyboarding the user story. Decide on the best ideas from Crazy Eights to proceed with.

The storyboard is then subjected to silent critique—everyone does "dot voting" on the ideas without really talking to others. Since there is no attribution to anyone's ideas, there is no "pressure" to accept the CEO's idea, for example. At the end, you get a heat map of what the group considers as the best ideas. Next, the team comes together and for each of the "hottest" ideas does a three-minute critique on what they like about the idea, what is missing, and so on.

Finally, the team does a super vote to choose the very best ideas. Repeat the process for any other idea that needs to be validated in the sprint.

Day 3: Decide

By the beginning of Day 3, you have come up with some great ideas. However, you have just a day to prototype them, so you must decide which of these ideas gets your "prototyping dollars."

Although voting might seem like the easiest way to decide which ideas to choose, groupthink can sometimes cloud a team's ability to choose the best ideas. The role of the facilitator becomes very important here. Looking for conflicts is a great opportunity to dig deeper into various options.

Finally, you have to make a key decision—whether to test out a single bold bet ("Best Shot") or have two equally appealing possibilities that you can't quite decide between and make them fight against each other ("Battle Royale"). Both strategies offer unique opportunities and are well suited for different situations, so the team needs to carefully evaluate those options.

Finally, you are ready to construct the entire storyboard to show just how the user will navigate each of the interfaces click-by-click.

Day 4: Prototype

Day 4 is the day when you get to "build" stuff to show to real users and get some meaningful feedback. However, all we have is one day to build a prototype to put in the hands of users so they can give us feedback on our key hypotheses.

To best utilize the validate stage (on the following and the final day of the sprint), we don't need high-pixel-quality prototypes. Some of the best prototypes are, in fact, built using Keynote and other simple tools. The idea is to avoid (or minimize) writing code as much as you can while making the prototype look as real as possible—what users really care about.

The team works together to produce a working prototype that will meet its first big test on Day 5.

Day 5: Validate

The last day of the sprint is important—it's where the rubber meets the road. The users whom you enlisted earlier are now raring to go; their feedback will be critical to your further progress.

Validation marks the end of a design sprint where a key hypothesis is collectively decided upon by the team and, through a series of divergent and convergent thinking steps, a prototype is made, which is then subsequently tested by "real humans." Given the track record of Google Ventures in applying design sprints to solve some hard problems, it offers a great way to align the team and make tangible progress in a short time period.

Customer Development, Lean Startup, and Business Model Canvas

Design thinking takes the entire process of prototyping into a close-ended process that starts with acquiring a deep knowledge of empathy about the target users rather than solving the problem using technology alone. It allows starting in the absence of any real input on what the intended solution might be. However, what do you do once you have zeroed down on the idea? Do you now go out and build the final product?

Well, not quite!

We still haven't quite figured out all the unknowns of the idea and the intended solution. We still need to systematically perform tests before we offer the idea as a full-scale commercial product. For example, until this point in our journey of the evolution and exploration of an idea, we haven't really figured out how are we going to make money. What if we built the product and offered it at a price point that was way above customers' expectations. Will it be way too late in the day to get that feedback? Or, how do we determine if the best way to reach our customers is through direct sales or through affiliate marketing? Pricing might only be one of the unknowns in the whole equation, and we might need to understand more about the market, target customers, value proposition, channels, and so on. Without fully understanding and validating these unknowns, building a product and simply relying on marketing push-and-sales gimmicks might be too risky. Apart from the risk of losing the investments and time, there might be a real risk to losing the market window.

Traditionally, product developers have often assumed that we know who the customers are, what the problem is, and what solution the customers desire. Unfortunately, most businesses make these one-sided assumptions that go untested for quite a while. When they get the shiny new product to market, they are often shocked to see there is no customer for their products!

Steve Blank has identified the need to "develop" customers in a similar fashion as we develop products—start with several hypotheses and rigorously test them until we have found the right answers. Only then can we begin to offer the idea as the full-scale solution. Blank has compiled his ideas in the "Customer Development Model." (See Figure 3-8.)

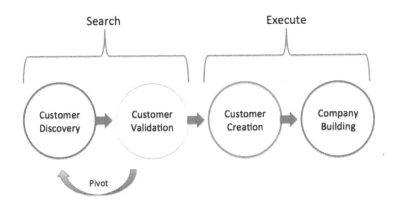

Figure 3-8. The Customer Development Model

In the initial stages, the customer development model talks about "searching" a repeatable and scalable business model. At that time, a new business or a new product doesn't know how to make money. The creator asks, "Who are my customers? What do they want? How will I serve them?' What are my cost structures?" and so on. Through a series of experiments, the teams find their business model that has no more hypotheses around it—all the unknowns and assumptions have been comprehensively tested and they are all ready for the next phase of execution. That's the time when we essentially step into the world of execution and scaling up.

The Customer Development Model starts with "Customer Discovery", where the focus is on understanding the problem and how a solution fits into it. The idea is not to develop a complete solution at this point, but to develop the minimum viable product that focuses on the "vital few" elements of the solution without too many finer details. Though the name "MVP" tends to limit the thinking to the "product," the product under question is the entire business model and not just the physical product that people buy.

Having identified, or discovered, the customers and having understood the "problem-solution fit," we then go on to the next stage of "Customer Validation" to validate how our proposed product fits in the market. At this point, we start sketching elements of the entire business model and design experiments that allow us to rigorously test the hypotheses until we have discovered the repeatable and scalable business model. When the assumptions prove to be invalid, as they indeed will, we go back and "pivot" on our business model, which essentially means we stay focused on the vision but change the strategy. Given that the focus is on learning, we are constantly willing to adapt to feedback that doesn't conform to our original hypotheses.

Only after we have eliminated all these unknowns and luck factors that might bring occasional success but not assure repeatability and scalability of the business model do we start building the machinery to create customer demand and offer a standard product. During this "Customer Creation" stage, we focus on scaling the execution, and we might undertake a series of activities to create the demand, build a sales playbook that allows us to scale up based on the proven patterns of successful lead generation and closure, and so on.

During the final "Company Building" stage, we eventually start scaling up the operations to sustain offering the entire business model in the most efficient and effective manner.

The entire Customer Development Model identifies several new ideas that have now evolved into disciplines by themselves.

One of the most interesting developments happened when Blank's student, Eric Ries, took the ideas around building MVP and published the book *Lean Startup*. His book identifies some very powerful—and radical—ideas to build new products by systematically and incrementally validating them before moving to the next stage. Another author, Alexander Osterwalder also wrote a very interesting book, *Business Model Generation*, which captures the essence of the business model in the context of entrepreneurship in a handy "canvas" format known as the "business model canvas." More specifically, it helps us examine elements of an idea not at the technical or the functional level, but at the entire business level. The ideas behind the business model canvas are coupled with the ideas of lean startups to create a powerful way to build new products by using the power of data-driven feedback. This facilitates "validated learning" that gradually raises the chances of eventual success.

Let's examine each of these ideas.

Business Model Canvas

Every business, new or old, startup or established, digital or conventional, product or service, has nine essential building blocks that describe key attributes about its business model:

1. **Customer Segments (CS):** Making a product that seeks to serve every conceivable customer segment might end up leaving everyone unsatisfied. Hence, every business must ask, "Whom are we serving?" Over time, a business might expand its footprint to address more than more customer segments, but in the lean startup world, it is recommended that we initially focus on only the most important customer segment.

2. **Value Proposition (VP):** Offering a "me too" product at a lower price point compared to incumbents might help you enter the market and be noticed, but might not be a sustainable growth strategy. Hence, each business must identify what really separates them from other competitors. Product traits like extended functionality, improved performance, interoperability, personalization, longevity of products, usability, and so on, are all examples of what might constitute a value proposition.

3. **Channels (CH):** There is no single way to reach the target customers; each way has its own pros and cons. Thus, a business must decide how do deliver its value proposition to the customer segments. For example, some of the leading Indian e-commerce sites, Myntra and Flipkart, have decided to go mobile-only, given the burgeoning mobile usage in Indian market.

4. **Customer Relationships (CR):** Depending on the product and specific customer segments, each business must identify what kinds of relationships it wants to establish with its customers. For example, most travel and hospitality companies have multiple touch points, and any bad experience can create upset customers. Consequently, such companies find a higher value in creating extensive loyalty programs that create multiple points of customer engagement, compared to, say, a laptop, where it is easy to compare specs by putting laptops side by side, and, hence, a relationship might end at the point of sale.

5. **Revenue Streams (R$):** Simply stated, no business can sustain indefinitely without having a solid revenue stream with its pricing mechanisms. Even businesses that offer "free" products must eventually have some form of revenue stream to stay afloat. While a site like Yahoo! might appear to have no apparent revenue stream to its end users, it needs to generate revenue from advertisers. Similarly, a business like Wikipedia must rely on donations to keep it going.

6. **Key Resources (KR):** Depending on the nature of the business and the type of product offered, a business might need different key resources to build its value proposition and offer it to the target customers. A business like Amazon doesn't really produce any of the products it sells, but needs extensive resources with supply chain, procurement ,and service delivery. On the other hand, for a company like IDEO, the key resources are its people who help solve complex problems by applying interdisciplinary skills.

7. **Key Activities (KA):** What are the key activities that a business must undertake to create, deliver, and sustain its value proposition to the customer segments? A company like UBER doesn't need to buy and operate a fleet of cabs, but simply have a way to onboard independent cab drivers. On the flip side, a company such as Apple must make heavy investments in R&D and design and develop new products. In addition, it must work with companies like Foxcon to produce iPhones. Each of these companies represent different key activities to its respective customer segments.

8. **Key Partnerships (KP):** What kind of partner and supplier ecosystem enables a business to offer value proposition in the most effective manner? Several other Japanese companies practice "keiretsu," which is a network of companies with deep partnerships that often result into shareholdings, and lead to shared learning and improvement. On the other hand, a small business might find value from signing up with someone like Amazon or Staples for taking care of its business needs.

9. **Cost Structure (C$):** What are the input costs in creating, delivering, and sustaining the value proposition? Some businesses like Intel's fab plants might need heavy upfront investment (including a long lead time) and run heavy risks in terms of anticipating future demand, while business like Wal-Mart might decide on keeping low prices and accept profits as low as 3% and, thus, have a different cost structure.

Normally, these elements are captured in a document like a business plan. Alexander Osterwalder took these nine building blocks and organized them into a one-page visual "canvas" in his book *Business Model Generation*, as shown in Figure 3-9.

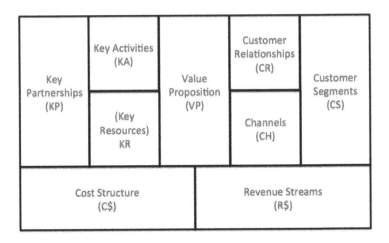

Figure 3-9. The business model canvas

The visual format makes it easy to capture the essence of several moving parts in order to view them holistically rather than seeing them as independent aspects of a traditional business plan spread over several pages.

The layout of these building blocks is not random. It depicts clustering of elements that provides value to the customers on the right side of the canvas and clustering of elements that identify efficiency on the left side of the canvas, as shown in Figure 3-10.

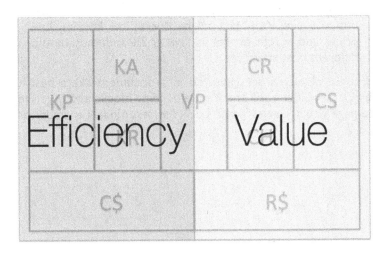

Figure 3-10. The business model canvas creates a balance between value and efficiency

Normally, these building blocks are identified in a document such as a lengthy business plan, but it tends to be rather dull and boring—and quite useless, given that a new business has absolutely no clue on any of these elements. At best, we make some convenient assumptions that mostly go untested as the team goes about building the entire product. Only when the full and final product is out in the market, do we actually start validating these assumptions. Needless to say, it is way too late to get validation feedback at that point, especially if major changes are needed because we made incorrect assumptions in the beginning.

To mitigate such risks, the business must identify some intelligent options and test them iteratively until each assumption on a business model canvas has been comprehensively validated and has eliminated any "luck" factor. Put another way, this is the stage at which all the cause-and-effect relationships between any elements on the business model canvas have been discovered and rigorously tested by field tests. (See Figure 3-11.)

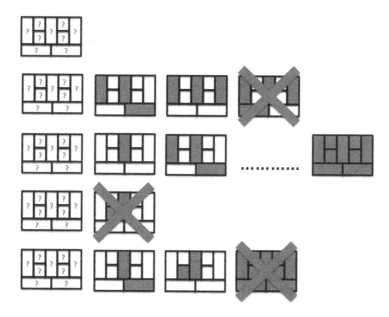

Figure 3-11. Validation of the business model canvas eventually leads to the one where all assumptions have been validated

The team starts with a set of business model canvases that might have different assumptions about different elements of the business model. They design the so-called "Minimum Viable Product" (MVP) that allows them to test and validate those assumptions using the least amount of time, effort, and money in learning cycles known as "build-measure-learn" loops.

An MVP is something that doesn't simply test the "product" as the technical product, but rather the entire business model! We clearly don't want to limit ourselves in validating all the unknowns. The term "MVP" connotes a small intersection between the terms "minimum" and "viable." It metaphorically represents the "vital few" as opposed to the "trivial many." Applying the central idea behind Pareto Law, we want to build and test that 20% of the product, which represents 80% of the value or risk, or both, to the central idea. (See Figure 3-12.)

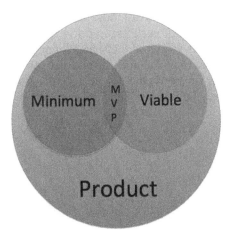

Figure 3-12. An MVP focuses on the "vital few" elements of the product that represent highest value or risk

The MVP allows the team to rigorously test its riskiest assumptions. Clearly, the goal is to limit how much finished product to build, but it is also important not ship a shoddy and incomplete product to the customer. We also want to test the hypothesis around revenue streams and the pricing mechanism, and not just the value proposition. If the product resembles a science project, the users might not "buy" it and the entire experiment might fall flat. On the other hand, to make the users "buy" a partial product, we can't simply go to the regular, or the mainstream, customers! They want the full and final product and nothing less, especially when they are going to pay for it! So, whom do we reach out to for feedback on our MVP?

In his 1962 book, *Diffusion of Innovations*, Everett Rogers identified how new ideas are spread. (See Figure 3-13.) He also identified a special category of users—he called them "innovators"—who are more interested in new ideas than any other cohort. These 2.5% of users are extremely "venturesome" due to a "... desire for the rash, the daring, and the risky."

34%
34%
13.50%
16%
2.50%
Innovators
Early Adopters
Early Majority
Late Majority
Laggards

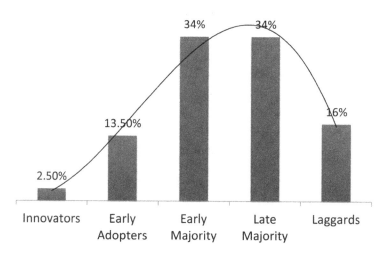

Figure 3-13. Innovators lead the pack when it comes to the diffusion of innovation

Rogers acknowledged the "gatekeeping" role these innovators play in the flow of new ideas into a system.

Steve Blank defines these innovators further as "earlyvangelists." (See Figure 3-14) and identifies them based on certain scenarios.

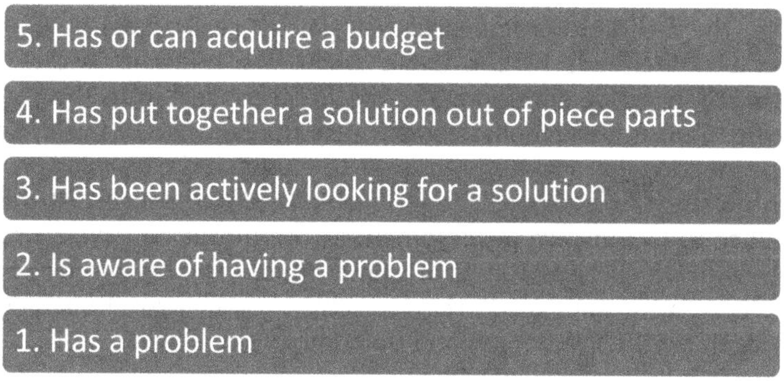

5. Has or can acquire a budget
4. Has put together a solution out of piece parts
3. Has been actively looking for a solution
2. Is aware of having a problem
1. Has a problem

Figure 3-14. The "Earlyvangelists" are great for validating an MVP

These early + evangelists, or earlyvangelists, not only have a much higher risk appetite, but they also have special knowledge about the problem that makes them not just passive consumers but also active co-creators. The best businesses learn how to leverage such specialized knowledge and skills into building great products and services.

Once we have identified the earlyvangelists, and have built the MVP, we subject it to experiment in the so-called "Build-Measure-Learn" cycle, as shown in Figure 3-15.

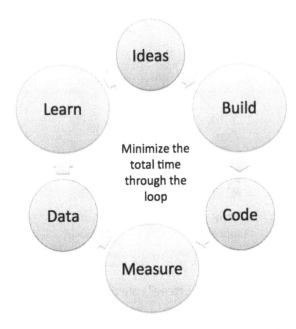

Figure 3-15. In a "Build-Measure-Learn" cycle, the idea is the minimize the time and effort to create learning about ideas

In essence, the Build-Measure-Learn cycle is not really new. At its core, it is the same as Deming's PDCA Cycle[6] but more relevant to the context of modern-day product development. The need to "minimize the total time through the loop" is also emphasized because the purpose of this cycle is not to ship the functionality sooner, but rather to expedite the learning process, in other words, facilitate a way to get actionable feedback sooner. At this point, we introduce agile software development as the means to develop software iteratively and incrementally in short time boxes. This allows us to design and implement experiments to progressively test each hypothesis before we decide to step up the investment and build the entire system.

---

[6]Initially known as PDCA cycle, it is also known as PDSA cycle. https://www.deming.org/theman/theories/pdsacycle

These ideas complement and reinforce each other, and allow us to establish checks and balances to systematically mitigate risks around each of the nine blocks of the business model. Gradually, we can scale up the level of investment to commensurate with the certainty and merit of the idea.

Lean Canvas

Ash Maurya made some changes to the business model canvas to adapt it specifically for products, and called the new canvas a "lean" canvas.[7] (See Figure 3-16.)

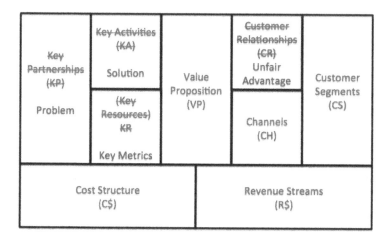

Figure 3-16. A lean canvas is an adapted version of the business model canvas

The lean canvas focuses on more specific elements at the product level than at the business level, and it could be the next step in evolution and validation of the product idea.

Figure 3-17 shows the new lean canvas.

[7]http://practicetrumpstheory.com/why-lean-canvas/

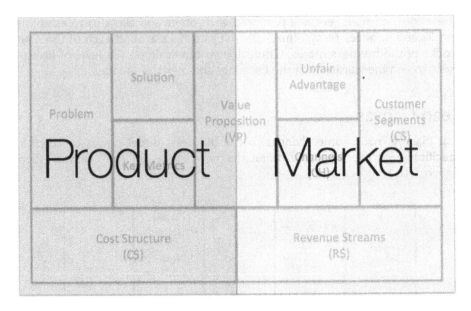

Figure 3-17. A lean canvas creates a balance between the product and market fit

It offers interesting alternatives to the business model canvas that explain more about the product-market fit. Thus, it is possible to build a product that understands and addresses the real needs of its intended audience. A lean canvas could be created and taken through the build-measure-learn loop and, when all its assumptions are validated, the team might achieve product-market fit. This marks the customer validation in the customer development model, and at this point, we are ready to move into the customer creation phase as part of the execution.

Conclusion

In the past, if an idea was considered cool, the next logical step was to build it and prepare for a full-blown, go-to market product with a grand product launch. However, this approach is fraught with risks, especially in today's "VUCA" world.[8] Furthermore, businesses no longer have the risk appetite to invest in multiyear research-and-development budgets and wait for the miracle to happen!

---

[8]VUCA stands for "Volatile, Uncertain, Complex, and Ambiguous."

Today, time and budgets are scarce, while ideas abound! However, simply having an idea or executing it mindlessly does not guarantee success. While execution is key, it makes sense to incubate ideas in a manner that aligns further investment with the amount of learning we have about the certainty, merit, and utility of the idea.

While having the next big idea is imperative, it is often hidden among hundreds of mediocre and worthless ideas. Employees often come up with countless ideas that go ignored in the absence of a mechanism to test them in a short amount of time with relatively little effort. Even the ideas that get validated don't often get end-user validation, and the result is a technical solution that might have no takers. We need to validate ideas for their commercial viability before we commit a large amount of time and money to it.

Describe

Let me tell you what I want ...

We are searching for some kind of harmony between two intangibles: a form which we have not yet designed and a context which we cannot describe.

—Christopher Alexander, American Architect

In the last few chapters, we have discussed how we go from mining ideas to systemically testing them until we have found a repeatable and scalable business model. Once we have the idea tested at a high level for its merit and feasibility and we understand the nine building blocks (Chapter 3) of its business model, we can begin to flesh out more details. Now that we've gone from the idea to prototype to MVP, the next logical step in this journey is to create the actual product, which needs to be developed over several iterations and releases. To accomplish this, we first need to be able to describe what we want! If we leave the description open-ended, we might be able to get started sooner, but we risk creating a product that might be too removed from the original idea. On the other hand, if we describe every single detail, we might take an inordinate amount of time, in which the market might change. We also risk making a very limited product that might not be able to benefit from creative ideas that, at a later date, could actually make the product much better. So, it makes sense to gradually evolve the idea into a tangible product with the details commensurate with the level of investment and decision-making.

Once we have deliberated on the right set of ideas and converged upon the most promising ones, we need to find a way to productize them. At the highest level, there could be issues relating to financial viability and ROI, or market fitment and future strategy. There could be decisions pertaining to technology, usability, internationalization, feature set, timelines, build vs. buy, and so on.

In this chapter, we will explore how we apply principles of agile software development to productize ideas so that we can accelerate product creation, mitigate product risks, and keep learning actionable through the journey.

Old-School Documentation

In traditional waterfall-based development, it was common for product managers to work alone and, after a couple of months of isolated work, come up with a big fat document called the PRD (Product Requirements Document), which would, in principle, capture everything that a customer might want in the upcoming product release. The product managers might gather inputs from sales, marketing, customers, support, engineering, and so on, but the process predominantly focused on having a phased approach to capture all the possible product requirements without the need to revisit them. Despite knowing the limitations of being able to forecast future needs accurately and precisely, and the futility of formalizing what can at best be described as a moving target, traditional organizations continue to practice such an approach. In some cases, this obsolete and largely farcical process is front-ended by marketing's period of intense activity where the output known as the MRD (Marketing Requirements Document) is created. An MRD might set the high-level context for the next several releases essentially based on a one-time market research—never mind that the market might evolve faster than the document might have predicted!

Traditional waterfall methods heavily relied on the power of documentation as the sole mechanism to describe ideas. However, no amount of documentation for a non-trivial system could possibly be comprehensive, complete, consistent, and correct all at the same time! Indeed, in several situations, we might actually be better off without any documentation, though we might need experts and a bit of luck, and our ideas might not constitute a "repeatable" process by any definition.

However, in reality, we do need a balanced approach. Some documentation rather than zero documentation or over documentation—could provide clarity about the intent and the desired outcome of an activity. It could quickly "validate" the high-level direction. Unfortunately, we often quickly lose the forest for trees.

Let's explore how agile thinking helps us articulate various aspects of a product that address increasing level of details as we make further progress.

Product Vision

Building a product is a transformational activity. It often changes how people, societies, and civilizations behave. Amazon has forever changed the way we buy books (and increasingly other stuff) from the Internet. Skype, Facebook, and WhatsApp have changed the way people communicate. Uber is disrupting the taxi business. Bitcoin might eventually change how digital money is used in future. Hundreds of other bold ideas are forever changing the world. One idea at a time, one product at time.

However, having such a profound impact can't be purely accidental. The creators of these ideas had a clear vision. Like the proverbial North Star, a vision helps creators stay focused as they experiment with their idea, but the star stays high enough to remain largely "unachievable." If creators achieve their goal reasonably early in the journey, we would consider it too tactical—no longer a "vision."

In 1983, Toyota Chairman Eiji Toyoda gave a mission impossible to his team —build the best luxury sedan in the world, in the first attempt.[1] There were top-of-the-shelf engineering specs to go along with it (top speed of 155 mph, 22.5 mpg fuel economy, and aerodynamic drag coefficient of less than 0.3—all these were unprecedented for a luxury sedan, let alone all being present in the same car). After six years and some 450 prototypes later, Lexus LS400 launched. Would Toyota have achieved such an unprecedented level of design and engineering excellence if not for such an audacious vision? What else could have sustained the untiring efforts and single-minded focus of 1,400 engineers over six years?

So, an important question is what the vision of the product is. Given that the basic technology in the majority of these examples is available, the question is not whether we can build it, but, rather, what should we build? In my view, a vision should be aspirational—even provocative—and the end-state of a product should be stated very crisply. Anything else is simply not a vision— maybe just a roadmap or even a to-do list.

> If you want to build a ship, don't drum up people to collect wood and don't assign them tasks and work, but rather teach them to long for the endless immensity of the sea.
>
> —Antoine de Saint-Exupéry

---

[1]"Shattering Expectations," Peter McSean, www.lexus-int.com/our-story/shattering-expectations.html.

In my view, a product vision should inspire people to long for the endless immensity of the sea, without actually prescribing how to go about building the ship. The vision might serve its purpose best by being minimalistic and inspirational.

Let's examine some of the way to articulate a great product vision.

Elevator Pitch

Popularized by Geoffrey Moore's classic *Crossing the Chasm*, the idea behind an elevator pitch is rather simple—can you explain your product in the time it takes to ride up in an elevator? Moore reasoned that venture capitalists don't invest in an idea if the creator can't pass the elevator test. If you can't pass the test, investors often make the following assumptions:

1. Whatever your claim is, it can't be transmitted by word of mouth.
2. Your marketing communications will be all over the map.
3. Your R&D will be all over the map.
4. You won't be able to recruit partners and allies.
5. You are not likely to get financing from anybody with experience.

Moore then prescribed a "proven formula" to guarantee passing the elevator test in just two short sentences:

For (target customers)

Who are dissatisfied with (the current market alternative)

Our product is a (new product category)

That provides (key problem-solving capability).

Unlike (the product alternative),

Our product (describe the key product features).

This formula is a simple template used even today to create a crisp positioning about the value proposition to your target investors. Its appeal lies in its simplicity, for anything that can be communicated in a hallway or at a water cooler has a better chance of being spread among the troops.

Product Vision Box

Each month, some 20,000 new consumer packaged goods are added from 50 countries to the world market.[2] This translates to almost 650 products a day!

Any guess how many of these actually succeed in the market?

Philip Kotler writes in *Principles of Marketing* that "of the 30,000 new food, beverages and beauty products launched each year (presumably in the U.S.), an estimated 70 to 90% fail within just 12 months." According to Jack Trout, a typical U.S. family buys only from the approximately 150 products that constitute 85% of its needs.[3]

How will you entice a consumer to pick up your product rather than any of the other competing products from the shelf? Despite all the evidence that suggests consumers are smart and intelligent and, hence, will find a way to choose better products, most are victims of old habits and don't always feel motivated to try new products outside the 150-odd products that serve the majority of their needs. So, how can you make someone interested in your new product? Having the lowest-priced product or trying some product-promotion gimmicks might get you some short-term attention, but if the customers can't relate to your product, chances are you will be heading back to the drawing board pretty soon. Here's where a product vision box could come in handy.

A product vision box is a visual and physical way to capture the most important aspects of the product that connect with customers. While it might appear to be a superficial packaging gimmick, especially if you haven't tried it before, the ability to drive a crisp, clutter-free message is perhaps an important part of the product positioning. You have very limited real estate on a physical product box (think of a "box" for dry cell batteries or maybe a bar of soap) and writing the entire PRD on the product box might be a sure way to drive customers faster to your competitor. On the other hand, if its packaging looks like it is missing important information, the product might fail to catch the attention of potential customers and miss the opportunity to tell its story. For example, Apple product boxes are known for their minimalistic design and uncluttered white background. Some other product boxes might be full of features and details, but these features and details might make the product seem cumbersome. The idea is to capture the most compelling set of product features that drive the right message across, and help a potential customer understand the product better, and expedite the buying process, ideally in your favor.

---

[2] www.gnpd.com/sinatra/gnpd/frontpage/?__cc=1.
[3] "Why Most Product Launches Fail," Joan Schneider and Julie Hall, https://hbr.org/2011/04/why-most-product-launches-fail.

Go ahead and try to create a product vision box. What will you write on it that will pique buyers' interest, perhaps enough to pick it up, check it out, and hopefully buy it? What are the top things that you will want your product to "say" to the buyers? To be able to do convey your product's features in a desirable way, you will need to have a deep understanding of your customers and their needs. By going through the process of getting to truly know your customers, you will come out with a much sharper vision of your story. While an elevator pitch might have gotten you started, a product vision box will make your story resonate with the actual buyers.

Check out Luke Hohmann's immensely useful book *Innovation Games* for details on how to go about playing the product vision box game. (Yes, that's what it is known as, and it already sounds interesting.)

Press Release

Amazon uses an interesting variant of the press release. Before even a single line of code has been written for a new product, its developers write a hypothetical press release and FAQ announcement.[4] By asking the team to come up with a compelling story, it helps uncover the key value proposition. It makes developers think of what features their potential customers would like to see in a product as well as what the most critical and unique value proportions are that trade journals and analysts would like to rave about. Thinking about a product while considering how to message it to customers makes the development team think about building the product from customer's point of view and not simply from the engineering point of view.

In his 2010 book about Amazon, *The Everything Store*, Brad Stone talks about this unique practice:

> Amazon's internal customs are deeply idiosyncratic. PowerPoint decks or slide presentations are never used in meetings. Instead, employees are required to write six-page narratives laying out their points in prose, because Bezos believes doing so fosters critical thinking. For each new product, they craft their documents in the style of a press release. The goal is to frame a proposed initiative in the way a customer might hear about it for the first time. Each meeting begins with everyone silently reading the document, and discussion commences afterwards.

---

[4]Here's the Surprising Way Amazon decides what new enterprise products to work on next – Jillian D'Onfro, http://www.businessinsider.in/Heres-the-surprising-way-Amazon-decides-what-new-enterprise-products-to-work-on-next/articleshow/46544156.cms.

While this style of product vision is a bit more verbose than the two previous ones, it requires thinking about the future and putting oneself in the customers' shoes. I would find it particularly useful to conduct such an exercise alongside your target customers—imagine being able to get direct feedback on your product from your target customers even before writing a single line of code.

Product Roadmap

A product vision is a high-level aspirational projection of the future state of a product. It must be impactful to generate sufficient interest among the innovators, early adopters, and early-stage investors. However, once it finds some level of interest and support, it must provide more details that reflect its conceptual integrity as well as a timeline outlining the introduction of features. What does each release look like, and when can the customers expect their favorite features? Here's where a product roadmap comes in handy.

A product roadmap is essentially a timeline of feature rollout plans. It helps product managers prioritize R&D dollars to maximize chances of realizing the product's promised or anticipated ROI. It allows the product team to focus on more value-creating features "here and now" versus hundreds of features that might have limited relative potential. And it helps customers know that their favorite features are planned somewhere down the road, and, if they so desire, the product team can expedite them.

The notion of "value" is often a poorly understood one. We all understand the intent of value but often struggle to articulate it in practical terms. It could be absolute or relative. An absolute value could be the real-dollar opportunity that exists if only a certain product or a feature were available by a certain time. Or, it could be the amount of money a customer is willing to pay to get some key feature. However, we might not always have a sense of the absolute value. The relative value is indeed a useful way to compare which of the features offers higher value. A simple tool to use is "Buy a Feature,"[5] where customers play with a notional $100 or $200 to buy the feature(s) they care about. Over a reasonably large sample of the target group, a clear pattern might emerge that helps identify which features are most valued. In *Innovation Games*, Hohmann has many such ideas to help prioritize features so that a product roadmap could be constructed or improved. One such game is the "20/20 Vision"[6] where the intent is to try to prioritize features relative to one another.

---

[5]www.innovationgames.com/buy-a-feature/.
[6]20/20 Vision, www.innovationgames.com/2020-vision/.

The notion of business value of software or a release must eventually be broken down at a feature, and eventually at a story, level. Indeed, this is among the most ill understood ideas in agile product development. In the waterfall world, the notion of business value at a requirement or a feature level didn't exist because so long as all features were delivered by a certain date, everything was of equally high value. Which is just a nice way to say that nothing was of value – at least on a relative basis. However, as we have seen from examples of MS Office 2007 and Instagram, it's clear that for just about any software product, not all features are alike.

Most people ignore close to 90% of the features and simply use features that meet their requirements. Since no team is blessed with an unlimited amount of time and effort, it makes no sense to mindlessly deliver all features in a waterfall manner. Instead, what does make software valuable is its ability to deliver the most important features.

Being able to articulate relative value helps a team understand the pecking order of requirements from an end-user's point of view, and is a great decision-making aid, especially when a team must prioritize its work (and later on, when it must constantly reprioritize its work to meet the project schedule and cost boundaries).

Using the notion of relative business value, a team could prioritize its work to maximize the "outcomes" and not just deliver the "outputs". I define outputs as simply the stories delivered at the end of an iteration, e.g., number of story points, or the velocity. It only signifies the throughput of a team's process. However, an outcome is much more, and I define it as the ratio of business value delivered by a story to its relative size. Note that both are abstract and relative quantities, and the notion of outcome is not a mathematically precise number but a way to order features in a consistent way such that a team is able to direct its effort in maximizing the outcomes over simply limiting itself to delivering higher output.

A product roadmap not only helps clarify how the R&D effort will be staggered to realize the product's vision and align the entire team around it, but it also allows customer feedback of what features are perceived as critical and what could be deferred to another time. In the case of B2B products, the roadmap allows (leads) customers to take on the role of active co-creators by letting them reprioritize based on the business needs. In the case of B2C products, the roadmap gauges potential interest from early adopters and thus ensures better ROI of the features.

My ideal view of a product roadmap is that it visualizes how a given piece of software will deliver outcomes over its entire development and sustaining cycle. However, most often, the product managers limit themselves to only identifying units of outputs (i.e., product features). While this might be a good starting point, it might be even more valuable to think of the product roadmap in terms of outcomes.

Product Backlog

The term "product backlog" comes from scrum methodology. A product backlog is a prioritized wish list of all features and bugs that a product owner would like to get implemented during the lifetime of a product. It differs from a product roadmap in the sense that a product roadmap typically doesn't have prioritized lists of features but might indicate a desired timeline (which might be more of a ballpark guess, as in Q3 or Q4) of them. However, a product backlog is not expected to have a timeline view, but just an ordering of features or requirements in terms of value to the customer.

The key distinction between a product roadmap and a backlog is about the confirmation of features in a given slice of time. While a roadmap might be more aligned to organizational boundaries, such as the annual budget, it might only have high-level bullet points about big buckets of functionality that are targeted to be delivered at big time intervals, typically each quarter, or so — but there might be no, or low commitment on all those features.

However in the case of a product backlog, the typical runway is for a release (and there might be potentially 2-3 releases in a year) and the features are linearly ordered in terms of priority. The timeline is not quite known, at least at the start of the release. The product backlog has a much shorter planning horizon than the product roadmap and hence is only expected to have more firm product feature requests, and, in turn, be assured more firm commitments by the development teams.

Product backlog is often described as being "DEEP":

- **Detailed appropriately:** The higher priority the features are in the backlog, the more likely they are known in greater details. This helps ensure we are not overspending our time and effort on features that are not important at this point.

- **Estimable:** If a backlog has features that appear to be too big to estimate, the team and the product owner work together to groom the product and bring it down to more acceptable levels.

- **Emergent:** This is a consistent theme across the whole of agile thinking—we recognize that we will get better clarity after we start the project. Sometimes new things will emerge, sometimes they will get clarified, prioritizes will change and so on. A product backlog is a live document that undergoes constant refinements.

- **Prioritized:** A product backlog must be able to provide direction about what is considered more valuable to its users so that the development team can focus its attention accordingly.

Note that there is no mention of size in the product backlog. In reality, a backlog undergoes a continuous process of analysis, refinement, and estimation—often known as "backlog grooming," or "story time." The result of such sessions is an increasing level of clarity about each of these features, a lowered sense of uncertainty, and a higher agreement within the team on its relative size—all of which helps improve planning and implementation of the respective features.

Sprint Backlog

Sprint backlog comes from the most popular agile methodology scrum (which is described in more detail in Chapter 6). It represents a subset of the highest priority requirements (and their component tasks) in a product backlog that have been mutually agreed upon by the product owner and the development team to be delivered in the current time box of planning and execution, known as "sprint" in scrum. These requirements are often initially bigger than what could be delivered in a single sprint and are sometimes known as "epic stories" or, simply, "epics." An epic that spans more than one sprint could represent both a technical risk (How are we going to implement and test it?) and a product risk (Is that what is really needed?) due to delayed feedback. Hence, it is generally broken down in what are known as "user stories" or, simply, "stories." Stories are normally small enough to be delivered in a single sprint, and they represent a finite amount of end-user facing functionality rather than a software module or a component that might exist independently but have no meaningful value from the customers' point of view.

A sprint backlog provides a common basis for the product owner and the team to plan and track their commitments over a short planning horizon that represents balance between the lowest risk in terms of the length of feedback loop and the impracticality and overheads of working in any timeslice smaller than that. The product owner makes plans for consuming the output of the sprint by organizing customer demos or customer betas, or simply dogfooding it internally. The team benefits by having a stable set of requirements that allows it to plan and organize its work without worrying about ad hoc planning or last-minute changes leading to task switching or rework. In addition, the output of a sprint is a collection of end-user facing sprints that help validate the entire technical stack, including integration of all software components. As a result, any risks relating to overall integration if performed towards the end get mitigated over time, with each sprint establishing a stable-state based on the incremental delta over the previous one. If the new state of the sprint is unstable or if the customer rejects the output of a sprint, the team can easily roll back to the previous sprint, which is the last-known stable state.

Scrum's rules prohibit making any changes to the sprint backlog once the sprint gets underway, so a scrum backlog is ideally created at the start of the sprint and then completed (or rather "burnt down") as the sprint progresses. If all its stories are completed and delivered as per their respective acceptance criteria, the scrum backlog is said to have been completed. Any leftover from the sprint backlog is simply moved back to the product backlog for reprioritization (not necessarily in the next sprint by default), and a fresh sprint backlog is created accordingly.

A sprint backlog allows creation of a "potentially shippable increment" of the most important features without worrying about the entire product backlog during a given sprint. This is important because it allows teams to make incremental progress while the product owner works on getting more clarity on the rest of the product backlog without really holding up the most immediate work. Any new requirements or changes are pushed onto the product backlog and prioritized by the product owner. During periodic backlog grooming sessions, the team examines the backlog. If it feels there is sufficient clarity, they estimate it so that the product owner can rearrange product release plans based on the objective and quantifiable data.

User Stories

"User stories," or simply "stories," is agile's preferred mechanism to create a placeholder for a future conversation between the product owner and the developers on a specific user requirement. Instead of spending too much time and effort to nail down every single detail about a product requirement upfront, agilists prefer to simply state the high-level functionality and let the details emerge from in-person conversations between the product owner and the developers at a time closer to its implementation.

In the process, time is saved from over documentation. The process also accommodates for leaving the implementation details until the last responsible moment and encourages the developers to think of creative solutions based on a high-level idea of what is required. Quite often, we get caught up in mechanics of stories, but miss the intent. The idea is not to capture and specify every single detail of the requirement (which would not only be too costly in terms of time and effort, but even be futile given the inefficacy of documentation to help clarify every possible detail, which anyway are likely to change over time), but to convey minimum yet adequate information about a feature for the purpose of high-level planning and technical analysis. The details are omitted for now. As opposed to the waterfall model, where all requirements are analyzed and designed well ahead of time, this is a very lean way of thinking about limiting the work-in-progress by doing only what the customer really needs. In addition, by delivering only the most valuable requirements, this model allows the delivery of working software rather than delivering documentation for all requirements, which might be of no significant value, especially to the customers.

User stories have a well-developed body of knowledge in terms of documenting them, writing them (for example, the "INVEST" test of readiness), or slicing them into smaller stories. However, simply visualizing them as an ordered one-dimensional list could make us see them as independent units of functionality with no relationships at a higher level. In his book *User Story Mapping*, Jeff Patton challenges developers to think of user requirements not only as a one-dimensional priority list as in a product backlog, but also as a two-dimensional map using cluster of product functionality as the second dimension. The developers can then build a "product" incrementally as opposed to focusing on disjoint features that might be delivered in the order of priority but might not reflect the needed functionality set. A story map can help in planning, implementing and delivering a product in terms of its functional completeness rather than simply delivering stories that might be ordered in terms of priority from a development team's point of view, but lack the meaningfulness from an end-user's point of view as a cohesive functional set. The user story map seeks to create an artifact that can bridge this gap, and provide a common basis for delivering functionality rather than being limited to an assortment of stories.

In my view, the journey of incremental development must begin with the ability to specify user requirements as bite-sized stories. If a product owner is not able to create such slivers of functionality, any ability to perform short-feedback agile engineering (such as TDD, refactoring, and CI) might simply be the raw horsepower that remains unharnessed. If one needs to eventually get to the point of continuous deployment, she must be able to think of product functionality in these terms. User stories provide a great mechanism to help get started.

Feature Prioritization

In my talks and presentations, I often ask what percentage of features people use with MS Word. The answers average between 10 and 15%. This range seems to corroborate well with a customer survey Microsoft did when creating MS Office 2007. When users of MS Office 2003 were asked what features they would like to have in MS Office 2007, more than 90% of them asked for features that were already present in MS Office 2003![7] It was a shame that they had not "discovered" them, let alone used them. If we could somehow

---

[7]https://news.microsoft.com/2006/11/21/microsoft-to-share-significant-ui-investment-in-2007-microsoft-office-applications-with-partner-community/.

learn what users want and find a way to deliver only those features (or deliver them sooner than the unimportant features), we might be able to create much higher value for our customers. Instead, we typically cram all the features in the products, thinking that we must compete feature-by-feature with competitors. Anything short of that is simply going to make our products inferior. Really?

Kathy Sierra, co-creator of the best-selling *Head First* series, hosts an influential blog known as *Creating Passionate Users*. In a blog post in 2005, "Featuritis vs. the Happy User Peak,"[8] she discusses the problem of product designers cramming way too many features into their product. She attributed that mindset to fear—the fear of being perceived inferior to competitors because of fewer features resulting in customers deserting them. As a result, we keep adding features until we come to the so-called "Featuritis Curve." Her hypothesis states that we should stop at the "Happy User Peak" stage and slow down on the development of new features. She argues that companies should focus on making a product or service easier to use rather than adding more features.

The question is how we prioritize the most important features so that we build just enough features and not overwhelm the consumer.

Back in waterfall days, prioritizing features was not a major prerequisite as long as 100% of the features were delivered by the promised date (but then it did lead to different problems by unnecessarily bloating up the software with 90% of the features being unwanted). The end-date was not only far out in future, but it also had enough hidden buffers due to the fundamental nature of waterfall planning. (We will discuss this in Chapter 6.) However, we never have enough time to deliver all the features, and even if we deliver them all, chances are high that not all features will be used. So, there needs to be a smarter way to focus on higher-value requirements before delivering the lesser requirements. Prioritization allows teams to make important trade-offs while directing their time and effort on activities that are more strategic or critical.

It is important to note that there might be different reasons to prioritize a given feature. For example, in some cases, delivering a high-value feature might be critical to demonstrate tangible progress to the customer, and it might be linked to some early cash flows. In some other cases, there might be a need to tackle the highest-risk items first in order to mitigate critical risks, say, around architecture or infrastructure.

A very simple way to prioritize requirements would be to somehow classify them as high, medium, or low priority. While there might be usefulness in such a classification, different people and different stakeholders might have differ-

---

[8]Featuritis vs. Happy User Peak, http://headrush.typepad.com/creating_passionate_users/2005/06/featuritis_vs_t.html.

ent understandings of each of these labels. We need some mechanism that is objective, transparent, and equally understood by all stakeholders.

Let's review some of the popular mechanisms to understand and prioritize product needs.

Kano Analysis

Not all features are equal! While some features create the so-called "wow" user experience, some features are simply table stakes—the presence of them doesn't add to user experience, though the absence of them could lead to customer dissatisfaction.

Professor Noriaki Kano developed the so-called Kano Model,[9] which helps place customer preferences into the following categories:

- Basic quality attributes are like table stakes, or hygiene factors: By themselves, they may not make a user happy, but their absence is likely to cause dissatisfaction. For example, a Bluetooth-enabled pairing of a smartphone with a car's music system is considered a standard accessory nowadays.

- Linear performance attributes are like a linear function: the more, the better. Examples include the battery life of a smartphone and the storage capacity of different models of a laptop.

- Exciters and delighters are the "wow" factors that make a product stand apart, and they might well be the competitive advantage the product offers. For example, today wireless charging of smartphones is a new thing and might be a very cool feature.

No feature remains static in its category. Over time, the exciters and delighters are copied by other competitors, and very soon they become table stakes. When Apple introduced the "pinch-to-zoom" interface for touch devices, it was revolutionary. Today, however, it is unimaginable for any device manufacturer to offer a touch product without it.

The Kano Model is a great visual tool to identify and describe different types of product features. If you have too many features in the basic or the linear performance category, chances are that you are not innovating enough. You might want to consider putting some time and money aside for creative thinking. On the other hand, if there are too many features in the exciters category,

---

[9]Kano Model, https://en.wikipedia.org/wiki/Kano_model.

you might run the risk of building a product so radical that the market might not be ready for it. Think of Amazon's Fire smartphone. With four front cameras, it offered the industry's first true 3D display. However, with no other perceived benefits over other comparable features, it bombed[10] at the market within a month of its introduction.

MoSCoW

You have a truckload of requirements to deliver, but you have a rather hard deadline to deliver them by. In most such cases, you might only be able to deliver some of those requirements. How will you decide what to deliver by the deadline? In many cases, we make either arbitrary and ill-informed decisions, or we simply go with the most demanding customers. However, this might not always be the best strategy. We need a more consistent way to categorize requirements into what must get shipped and what could be optional. While it might be ideal if all the features could be delivered, the reality is that we will always have more feature ideas than time! So, by focusing on the "must-have" requirements, we are able to address a minimal, usable subset of the business case that helps focus maximum effort toward it. Over time, other features will be addressed.

Originally developed as part of the DSDM method,[11] MoSCoW is a simple but useful technique to prioritize requirements based on their perceived relative criticality. It doesn't use any quantitative measures in coming up with a relative prioritization, but it allows the delivery of "Minimum Usable Subset" of requirements:

- **Must:** This requirement is mandatory, or a "must-have," for the final deliverable to be accepted. All requirements placed in the Must category must be included in the final delivery, for if even one is missing, it could mean total rejection of the final work product. Such a grouping is also known by the acronym MUST (Minimum Usable SubseT).

- **Should:** This is not a mandatory requirement, but it is included in the final deliverable if possible. It might represent a critical requirement, but something that might be possible to realize in some other way.

[10]Why Amazon's Fire phone failed, http://fortune.com/2014/09/29/why-amazons-fire-phone-failed/.
[11]www.dsdm.org/content/10-moscow-prioritisation.

- **Could:** This requirement might be considered "good to have" if time and money permits.

- **Won't:** This requirement is not required in the current version, but might be needed in a future version. The only reason to communicate it might be so that designers are consciously aware of any design implication to consider at this point (without really bloating the design for futuristic requirements).

Let's take an example. If you were designing a new smartphone, you might use MoSCoW to prioritize requirements, as shown in Table 4-1.

Table 4-1. Features Prioritization for a Smartphone

Priority	Features
Must	Make voice calls
	Surf Internet
	Check e-mails
	Pre-loaded apps for alarm, contacts, calendar, music, videos, camera
Should	Download new apps
	Allow documents to be stored locally to read later
Could	Waterproof
	Wireless charging
Won't	3D display
	Word processor

Creating a prioritization along these lines can allow users and developers to be on the same page, and it helps focus on core value features, especially when time is at a premium.

Financial Measures

Every product can be considered as a series of cash flows in finance terms. There could be an initial investment upfront (meaning, "outflows") in terms of acquiring hardware or software or buying some infrastructure or tools, followed by periodic outflows. This could go on for some time until the product is ready to be shipped. When customers start paying for it, there could be cash "inflows." Eventually, we break even when we have recovered all the initial investment. Then we start making profits.

Typical cash outflows include salaries for product team, bills for utilities (such as facility rent, electricity, water, and networking), development tools, licensing fee, servers, training budget, marketing budget, sales costs, and so on.

Typical cash inflows could include revenue from sales, royalty payments, licensing revenues, lead generation commission, and so forth.

In this simplistic model, we could envisage each product and its features as various financial measures. For example, a product might need an upfront investment of $100k and start giving returns of $50k in the third year. It will then provide a lifelong return of $10k. Maybe there is another product that needs $200k investment upfront and only starts returning in the fifth year, but it returns $30k every year. Which product is a better investment?

There are several measures that can help us make such product decisions using financial measures, when such data is available. These mechanisms are often used in portfolio management but could also be used when big-ticket features need to be decided. Let's look as some of these measures.

Break-even Period (BEP)

A break-even period (BEP), or the payback period, is simply the amount of time it takes to recover all investments. In most cases, we want the quickest BEP. However, these might be businesses that have a long gestation period and, hence, have a long BEP. For example, Peter Thiel in his 2014 book *Zero to One*, says "…most of a tech company's value will come at least 10 to 15 years in future." He is referring to "value" and not the BEP, but if we extend the idea of how long it takes to recover the "value", we can draw comparisons. Talking specifically about the company he co-founded, PayPal, he says most of the company's value will come from 2020 and beyond. Clearly, when you are building a great product or a great company, you are not looking for a quick way to make money and exit out. On the other hand, an extraordinary long BEP could also make investors worry if the business is interesting enough. So, a balance might be needed, but being aware of the BEP might be a good starting point before making the decision.

Internal Return Rate (IRR)

Any investment made by a company might require that the product deliver returns higher than a given minimum rate of return, often known as the "hurdle rate." This might be a company's internal discipline to invest in products that deliver a certain minimum ROI. A product with a high IRR might reflect a market opportunity to offer premium services, whereas one with a low IRR might reflect a highly commoditized market where cost is the only differentiation and hence a focus on offering basic hygiene features in the most cost-effective manner might be the only strategy till a firm can figure out how to create some form of value differentiation. For example, a firm might consider the Blue Ocean strategy to offer value without necessarily succumbing to price leadership which might only create a "me too" product and offer no real innovation.

Discount Cash Flow (DCF)

A discounted cash flow takes macroeconomic factors such as rate of inflation into account to offset the true time-value of money. Compared to a regular cash flow analysis, a DCF makes a more realistic comparison of cash flows.

Net Present Value (NPV)

The net present value is the sum total of all the product's cash inflows and outflows, and it is typically discounted against inflation. It is one of the most common measures to compare between two financial instruments. Warren Buffet is supposed to use NPV to decide on investing in companies.[12]

Cash Cycle

A cash cycle is a simple, but extremely important measure of the amount of time between the point when we start collecting money from customers and the time we pay our suppliers. A negative cash cycle, thus, is not a mathematical fallacy, but a great business acumen. It basically means that you collect money from customers first and then pay your suppliers later, and it represents virtually no need for the working capital (which, if anything, is negative here). Working capital is another form of the inventory, and the longer the sales cycle, the more working capital is needed to remain inside the system, thus representing a higher amount of inventory. Thus, a negative cash cycle means there is literally no such inventory. Companies such as Toyota and Dell have created an extremely efficient lean production system to build products only against firm order (MTO, or Made-to-Order) rather than the conventional methods of mass-producing products against forecast (MTF, or Made-to-Forecast). The MTF approach keeps high inventory locked up until the time the final sale happens, and it carries the risk of not having demand as per the plan. Amazon had a cash cycle of -14 days in 2012[13] and it means there is virtually no need to hold cash to operate such a business.

---

[12]A Refresher on Net Present Value, https://hbr.org/2014/11/a-refresher-on-net-present-value.
[13]The Cash Conversion Cycle, http://www.forbes.com/sites/ycharts/2012/03/10/the-cash-conversion-cycle/.

Inventory Turns

Inventory turnover, or simply inventory turns, is another very interesting measure of the efficiency of the end-to-end process of product development and sales. It is an indicator of how many times a company's inventory gets sold and replaced over time. A high inventory turnover means there is a strong demand for sales and a corresponding lower amount of inventory of unsold goods, which results into lower risk of stock surpluses. On the other hand, a low inventory turn could represent a sluggish demand for the product (for whatever reason) and might represent a higher amount of unsold goods, leading to risks around it.

Apple is thought to have 74 inventory turns in a year, which is the highest in the industry.[14] This means Apple turns over its entire inventory every five days (and only McDonalds with 2.5 days fares better than Apple). In lean terms, it represents an extremely low amount of inventory in the process.

Pugh Matrix

Let's consider a situation where there are several options, but we can only choose one of them. Let's also consider that there are multiple factors that we can use to compare these options—so, there is no one single factor that can be chosen as the tiebreaker. These factors may again not have the same relative importance. How do we decide which option is "better" than the others?

Stuart Pugh created the "Pugh Matrix,"[15] which is a simple way to identify factors, allocate weightages, and weigh each of the factors against the parameters so that a weighted sum is available for each option. The option with the highest weighted sum would then be chosen as the best option representing the most balanced choice among all factors and their relative weights.

For example, a chief product owner might be faced with the choice of deciding between multiple product proposals. She might apply weightage to choose the most promising one, say, based on market size, newness of technology, propensity to pay premium prices, and distribution costs. Based on the relative important of these factors for all the product proposals, their relative weights could be considered and a Pugh Matrix could be created for comparing various product candidates to arrive at a single decision.

---

[14]Apple turns over entire inventory every five days, http://appleinsider.com/articles/12/05/31/apple_turns_over_entire_inventory_every_five_days.
[15]Decision Matrix, http://asq.org/learn-about-quality/decision-making-tools/overview/decision-matrix.html.

Conclusions

Applying agile thinking to product development allows various product artifacts to be created with increasing level of detail as there is confirmation on the previous steps. This allows only investing the time and effort on the details that are needed here and now, as opposed to building everything in finer detail for a future that may or may not happen.

Various key artifacts can be thought of as multiple agile runways that have varying lengths, as shown in Figure 4-1.

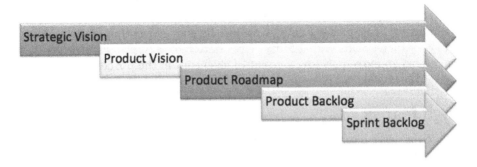

Figure 4-1. Product runways represent planning horizon at varying levels of operational details

The strategic vision of a company helps establish a long-term vision that aligns all its products in a common direction. This might be abstracted at sufficiently high levels and act as the common frame of reference to any product that gets built under a portfolio or inside the company. It has a rather long runway given its nature. A product vision acts as the true north for a specific product and might have a long-term runway for it, say between three and five years. A product roadmap could be zooming into the product vision and allocating it to some timelines, typically around an annual plan (because that tends to be the budgeting and revenue cycle in most organizations). Product backlog might refer to the next 1–3 releases, and the sprint backlog is the most specific and shortest runway among them all—just two to four weeks in most cases.

How do these artifacts help? To begin with, they allow us to make well-informed trade-offs between predictability and flexibility. In general, the longer the planning horizon, the higher its flexibility in accommodating changes. However, that flexibility comes at the cost of predictability. Similarly, the shorter the runway, the lower its flexibility in accommodating late changes, which lead to much higher predictability. This trade-off is represented in Figure 4-2.

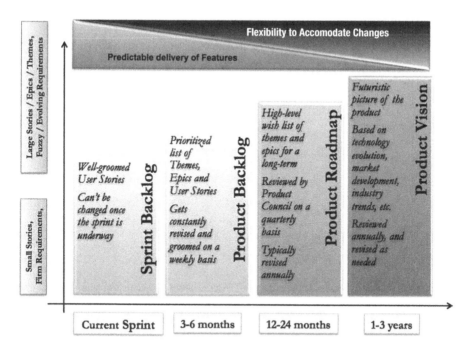

Figure 4-2. Product runways represent a healthy trade-off between flexibility and predictability

Starting with the long-term product vision, we have high flexibility in what is to be implemented to realize the product vision, but that have little or no predictability in when it will be delivered. This isn't necessarily bad because it is still early in the process. Once we have the necessary sign-offs on the vision, we can flesh out more details until we have very firm requirements that must go into the current sprint. This can offer a high level of predictability but at the cost of sacrificing flexibility. The idea is that in the coming two- to four-week period, we must have a very clear picture of what is really needed. By locking down those short-term requirements, we are able to raise predictability in our work.

Agile methods offer mechanisms and artifacts to capture and describe such nuances to aid progressive elaboration as the idea gets validated and evolves. As a result, we can build plans with increasing clarity and predictability. Note that at any time, changes can be accommodated. However, to ensure that unbridled changes don't disrupt the entire effort, agile methodologies such as scrum introduce some constraints that help maintain a healthy balance between flexibility and predictability.

In Chapter 5, we will discuss how an agile team incorporates these product descriptions in designing and developing a product.

Design

Design is how you design!

Design is not just what it looks like and feels like. Design is how it works.

—Steve Jobs

This is the golden age of design. We have gone past the point where products compete on functionality alone. Today, most products easily meet our basic needs in terms of functionality. Most washing machines offer similar basic functions, and the same can be said about cars, smartphones, wrist watches, word processors, or just about any other modern-day product. Similarly, every web-mail or cloud storage service offers similar features. Sure, there are clever innovations related to making some features stand out from others and to using an intellectual property to protect from (and outcompete) the imitators, but the basic function of these products and services are dangerously alike. Even price points are within the same ballpark. In such a world, how do you create products that stand out from your competitors?

In context of agile product development, the notion of architecture design undergoes a major paradigm shift. Agile methods favor an "inspect-and-adapt" approach that is based on a working software being subjected to a real-world deployment. The traditional approach, on the other hand, was to "slow cook" in the sense that a lengthy document was created to diligently document all aspects of design in adequate detail that would then be reviewed to verify its correctness and other non-functional aspects such as performance, scalability, reliability, portability, and maintainability.

In this chapter, let's look at some of the ideas behind design, and the methods and practices that designers use to accomplish these objectives.

Design as Differentiator?

In a world where everyone is constantly copying each other, how do you create a niche and be seen as the preferred choice by your customers? In other words, why should your customers choose you over your competitors?

Could functionality, or rather more functionality, be the differentiator? While an incumbent might have the unfair advantage of having more product features (apart from knowing the market and the customer needs better), having more features alone might not help a challenger. In fact, it might not even help the incumbent, either. Myspace was the market leader between 2005 and 2008 and even surpassed Google as the most visited web site in the United States in 2008. Yet none of its early popularity could save it from eventual extinction as Facebook gradually came up with a better product.[1] MP3 players (and the previous generation successes like music CDs) existed long before Apple introduced the iconic iPod, which offered hardly any new "functionality" in the traditional sense. The contemporary (and largely anecdotal) data seem to suggest that less functionality—not more functionality—might actually be a key factor in a winning product.[2] When burbn.com built a copy of foursquare.com as a check-in service app, they found that most people who were using their service were simply using it to upload pictures from their mobile phones. They created the "zoom-in" pivot and the resultant product, Instagram, created a billion-dollar value.[3] Perhaps Dave McClure's prescription to "kill a feature every week"[4] isn't that radical after all!

Could price perhaps be the differentiator? While the incumbent is sitting pretty with an uncontested market leadership and enjoying hefty profits, how does a challenger enter the ring and disrupt the market? Perhaps the answer is in offering a similar product at a lower price point. GM employed this clever strategy back in 1924. While Ford was sticking to a single model in each segment, GM came up with the idea of "a car for every purse and purpose."[5] That surely was a winning strategy for GM for the next several decades. However, with today's consumers spoiled by choice, a lower price point alone might not be the best strategy, especially if it makes the business itself unviable over

---

[1]Sean Parker, "Why Myspace Lost To Facebook," http://techcrunch.com/2011/06/28/sean-parker-on-why-myspace-lost-to-facebook/
[2]"Why More Features Doesn't Mean More Success," https://blog.kissmetrics.com/features-doesnt-mean-success/
[3]"How Instragrm Grew from Foursquare Knock-Off to $1 Billion Photo Empire," www.inc.com/eric-markowitz/life-and-times-of-instagram-the-complete-original-story.html
[4]"Startup Metrics for Pirates/KILL a feature," www.slideshare.net/dmc500hats/startup-metrics-for-pirates-fowa-london-oct-2009/17
[5]https://history.gmheritagecenter.com/wiki/index.php/1924,_%22A_Car_for_Every_Purse_and_Purpose%22

the long term, as the Kingfisher Airlines experience taught us.[6] Proclaiming itself as India's only five-star airline, Kingfisher offered top-of-the-shelf premium services and yet kept underpricing itself in the fiercely competitive and newly opened Indian aviation market. Having never made any profits during its lifetime, it finally stopped operations in 2012. Though its current state is unknown, it is most likely a closed chapter.

What other ways could a newcomer disrupt the market and win the market share? Let's consider a few examples.

When Apple launched the first iPhone in June 2007, market leader Nokia was worth $115 billion and Blackberry $40 billion.[7] Clearly, the iPhone was not a threat to them. Nokia's Chief Strategist Annsi Vanjoki is supposed to have made this statement:

> The development of mobile phones will be similar in PCs. Even with the Mac, Apple has attracted much attention at first, but they have still remained a niche manufacturer. That will be in mobile phones as well.[8]

Blackberry's maker, RIM, actually thought iPhone was impossible in 2007 and that Apple was lying about having developed it.[9] What stopped the traditional phone makers to think differently and disrupt their own success before someone else could?

Consider Uber. The idea for Uber was born on a snowy night in Paris when Travis Kalanick and his friend Garrett Camp couldn't get a cab. Garrett said, "I want(ed) to push a button and get a ride."[10] As a result of this experience, Kalanick and Camp decided to disrupt the market. Today, Uber has close to a million drivers working with it globally (and it expects to add another million in 2015 alone) and a valuation of over $50 billion.[11] Yet, it owns not a single car. (In fact, it actually wants to end car ownership all together and make the world a bit greener.) Uber reached the $50-billion milestone two years sooner than even Facebook did. No wonder Google wanted to invest

---

[6]"The Flight and Fall of Kingfisher Airlines, " www.livemint.com/Opinion/n62RtIr809UKqfgTJNDnIM/The-flight-and-fall-of-Kingfisher-Airlines.html
[7]"iPhone, Nokia, and Blackberry: One Chart That Tells a Story of Divergent Fortunes," https://gigaom.com/2013/09/26/iphone-nokia-blackberry-one-chart-that-tells-a-story-of-divergent-fortunes/
[8]"Top 5 Assclown iPhone Quotes in 2007," http://gizmodo.com/5416781/top-5-assclown-iphone-quotes-in-2007
[9]"RIM Thought iPhone Was Impossible in 2007," www.macnn.com/articles/10/12/27/rim.thought.apple.was.lying.on.iphone.in.2007/
[10]"5-Year Anniversary Remarks From Uber CEO Travis Kalanich," https://newsroom.uber.com/2015/06/5-years-travis-kalanick/
[11]"Uber Values at More Than $50 Billion," www.wsj.com/articles/uber-valued-at-more-than-50-billion-1438367457

in Uber so badly. Google literally gave Uber a blank term sheet![12] Why had none of the carmakers and rental companies in the world come up with such an outrageous idea?

Here's another example, this time from India. If Google truly disrupted the ad market in the Internet world, InMobi did that in the mobile world. It reached one billion unique mobile devices in February 2015, making it the largest mobile ad platform in the world[13] and second largest overall, second only to Google. InMobi started in India in 2007 when no one gave India a chance as it was predominantly a feature-phone market. (However, it will become the world's second largest smartphone market by 2017.)[14] Again, what stopped the existing (largely Western) Internet players to ignore this burgeoning market of the future, and what did InMobi do differently to become the global leader?

Did InMobi just build yet another mousetrap with more features, or did it sell its new product at lower cost? I don't think so. Did it build better products and services? I definitely think so.

Apple continues its relentless march to build better products through its highly secretive design process that Jony Ive summarizes as "design is the whole thing."[15] Uber wanted to make it simple for people to get a cab, and InMobi sought to ride the wave of mobile adoption in emerging markets and "completely understand the usage pattern and trends," which was being missed by the Western Internet-based companies.[16]

So, where does it all lead?

One common thread that unites these examples is how well these products and services are designed—not just the bright and shiny wrapper, but as a well-designed product in the truest sense. These companies aim to deliver superior experiences through their deep understanding of target group users rather than mindlessly stuffing features into the product. They strive to learn about their pain points and address them through evolving innovative solutions and by increasing the number of cases through "co-creation." They don't proceed with a "we-know-everything" attitude, but actually listen to their prospective users and aim to deliver solutions through a process of

---

[12]"Google Wanted to Invest in Uber so Badly, it Gave CEO Travis Kalanick a Blank Term Sheet," www.fastcompany.com/3050811/fast-feed/google-wanted-to-invest-in-uber-so-badly-it-gave-ceo-travis-kalanick-a-blank-term-

[13]"InMobi Reaches Over One Billion Mobile Devices," www.inmobi.com/company/press/inmobi-reaches-over-one-billion-mobile-devices/

[14]"India Will Pass US to Become World's Second Largest Smartphone Market by 2017," http://venturebeat.com/2015/07/01/india-will-pass-u-s-to-become-worlds-second-largest-smartphone-market-by-2017/

[15]"Apple's Jonathan Ive in Conversation with Vanity Fair's Graydon Carter," https://youtu.be/ef69BUlge-A

[16]"The 'InMobi' Story," http://headstart.in/2009/12/14/the-inmobi-story/

continuous feedback, adaptation, and improvement. They display the humility to accept feedback—as critical as it might be—so that they can take baby steps and deliver better products on an incremental basis. They don't simply deliver a technology and expect their users to start using it, but firmly position their users into the center of the process. They build their products for "real humans," and not for people like themselves who might have achieved a higher level of technology sophistication.

In short, they have all learned to design their products better on an ongoing basis. So, what is design?

What is Design?

In his 1988 classic *The Design of Everyday Things*, the design guru Dan Norman talks about the problems with the design of everyday appliances. He recounts that Kenneth Olsen, who founded Digital Equipment Corporation. "couldn't figure out how to heat a cup of coffee in the company's microwave oven," and goes on to argue that "you probably would need an engineering degree from MIT to work it." (Incidentally, Olsen had two degrees from MIT, and yet couldn't quite figure the microwave out!)

Why is it that some products are designed so badly that they actually end up annoying the users? In terms of functionality, they perhaps offer the same features as other products, but the way they are designed to deliver those functionalities leaves the users fuming. No wonder such products are simply stillborn when they are launched!

Is design an art form? Is it a science, a product of engineering, or, more increasingly in the context of building better products, yet another management discipline? I think of design as a field that requires multiple competencies from various disciplines, such as the arts, sciences, humanities, and engineering, to solve problems in a creative and useful manner. The end goals of a design can't just be the design in and of itself. (If it is, it might be closer to an art form, and while it might have a great artistic and aesthetic value, it might have a limited utilitarian value.) It also might not be just science that offers a great possibility inside the labs under "test conditions," but hardly holds up when exposed to the real world. It also can't be a just hardcore engineering solution that is so brilliant and efficient that it is probably not even usable by the fallible, ignorant, and unpredictable humans. Limiting it to humanities might fail to highlight the aspect of building a commercial product that uses technology to deliver the intended solutions. So, what, then, is design?

In his immensely readable book, *Design: A Very Short Introduction*, John Heskett defined design in a rather "nonsensical sentence":

> Design is to design a design to produce a design.

He identified design as the overall concept that entails using "design" as a verb. He also describes it as the process behind the overall concept. In addition, he indicates that "design" refers to some idea or concept being developed. Finally, Heskett suggests that "design" is the final, tangible outcome. He recognizes that design takes place at multiple levels.

We can say the same about design in the context of software products as well, and we can perhaps divide them into two broad themes.

At the outermost level, there is an element of external appearance and usability —the look-and-feel aspects, and the way a target user interacts with a given software. Design, or more specifically human-centered design (also known as user-centered design or "UCD," user experience or "UX," and often mistaken for a much smaller subset of the overall user experience known as the user interface or "UI"), is perhaps the single most important factor today in our post-Apple world. Consumers expect a very high level of usability and intuitiveness in products. They are often willing to forgo some aspects of functionality and even pay more for desirable products.

There are also hidden (but highly "visible" when done poorly) elements of the internal working of a software under the hood—how its data structures are used, how optimally the algorithms use computing resources, how various modules inside a system communicate with each other, and so on. For a large part, these elements relate to the fundamentals of computer science and are realized through the state-of-art technology available to its software designers. In this book, we limit ourselves to the first level of product design because we believe the topic of software design requires a much deeper and specialized discussion than the intent and scope of this book. However, we shall touch upon the topic.

Is every design good? We all have seen scores of products that are way too complex to be useful. Even if the original idea was brilliant, the way it is designed and executed leaves much to be desired. The world is full of such products. In fact, there are some interesting ones called out on a blog post on UXPin.[17]

So, what is good design and how do you recognize it?

What is Good Design?

Deiter Rams[18] is one of the most influential industrial designers, known for his "less, but better" philosophy to design. He was the Chief Design Officer at the German electrical appliances company Braun between 1961 and 1995, during which time he and his team designed over 500 products. The only other

---

[17]"10 Worst Design Failures of All Time," http://blog.uxpin.com/2837/10-worst-design-failures-of-all-times/
[18]www.vitsoe.com/gb/about/dieter-rams

company he worked with is British furniture maker Vitsoe, a company whose goal has always been to make long-living furniture.

In 1976, he delivered a talk[19] where he said "design is a popular subject today. No wonder because, in the face of increasing competition, design is the only product differentiation that is truly discernible to the buyer." I think that message is even more relevant today!

He described ten principles of good design.[20] Jony Ive, Apple's Chief Designer, considers Dieter Rams as his inspiration, and, in turn, Rams considers Apple to "genuinely understand and practice the power of good design."[21] I think that alone calls for a good reason to study his principles:

1. Good design is innovative.

   There might be several ways to solve a problem, and some of them are surely uglier than others. While we want to eventually solve the problem, we don't want to design the product so that it looks like it was accomplished with an obsolete technology. The design must evolve in tandem with newer technology and provide innovative solutions.

2. Good design makes a product useful.

   While good design is desirable, it is not the end in itself. Customers want to solve their problems, and they need a better and more useful product—the design must eventually lead to such a product. It is not just about functionality alone, but the design must also cater to the physiological and aesthetic aspects of the product.

3. Good design is aesthetic.

   A good design is a piece of art. Apart from its functional value, it appeals to our senses—be it visual, aural, or touch (and even smell and taste well!). I have thought of a simple test for an aesthetic design—place it in the hands of someone who hasn't tried the product before and leave it for 20 or 30 seconds while you talk about something else. In the meantime, let the person touch and feel the object. Then try to take it back—if the person doesn't part with it easily, you know you have an appealing product.

---

[19]"Dieter Rams: Design by Vitsoe," www.vitsoe.com/files/assets/1000/17/VITSOE_Dieter_Rams_speech.pdf
[20]"SFMOMA Presents Less and More: The Design Ethos of Dieter Rams," www.sfmoma.org/about/press/press_exhibitions/releases/880
[21]"Dieter Rams: Apple has achieved something I never did," www.forbes.com/sites/anthonykosner/2013/11/30/jony-ives-no-longer-so-secret-design-weapon/

4. Good design makes a product understandable.

   I am sure many of us can relate to seeing old VCRs in our living rooms that perpetually blinked "12:00" all the years we had them. Why didn't we just set them to the right time? Because, generally, people didn't have the patience to read the bulky and confusing user manuals,[22] or they were unable to intuitively figure out how to program their VCRs. A good design aims to do exactly reverse—build products that are easy to understand, making those useless user manuals obsolete.

5. Good design is unobtrusive.

   Good design must lead to purposeful products, which are like tools—they should be attractive but, apart from their usefulness, not demand unnecessary attention.

6. Good design is honest.

   When you use Dropbox, you experience honest design. This honesty is apparent when compared to Dropbox's ancestors (good old FTP software) where one had to go a character interface and do dozens of manual settings to correctly complete a simple file transfer. Dropbox doesn't trick the user or manipulate the user into operating it in a certain manner. Rather, it is very transparent (and easy) what to do.

7. Good design is long-lasting.

   LEGO blocks are a perfect example of a great design that is long lasting. If you have ever held one of those blocks in your hands, you probably didn't want to let it go. LEGO blocks not only look "inviting," but they are also extremely durable in both their appeal as well as durability. An average LEGO brick can be used 37,112 times!,[23] and perhaps the LEGO bricks made in 1950s can still be used with more moderns ones! A good design doesn't seek to cut corners in the name of creating something that is simple and visually appealing.

---

[22]Incidentally, Elon Musk believes that any product that needs a manual to work is broken.
[23]"LEGO's Magic Number Is 37,112," http://phillipecantin.blogspot.co.uk/2013/02/legos-magic-number-is-37112.html

8. Good design is thorough down to the last detail.

   In the 2013 movie *Jobs*, Steve Jobs (played by Ashton Kutcher) says, "We gotta make small things unforgettable." When an employee responds that "typeface isn't a pressing issue," he fires him on the spot. While this might have been an artistic portrayal of the enigma that was Steve Jobs, it must reflect his vision. We can see this vision when we look at Apple products of today living up to such high attention to "pixel-perfect" details.

9. Good design is environmentally friendly.

   There was an interesting article that argued if all industries (and not just the companies) were asked to factor in the cost of "natural capital," no industry would ever be profitable.[24] We must remember that the natural resources we use in building products must not pollute the environment. This is equally applicable to digital products, even when the resource is "invisible" (for example, power consumption or radio waves, or the amount of time people spend figuring out a feature).

10. Good design is as little design as possible.

    I believe Apple is perhaps the best embodiment of this minimalist principle. Its products are extremely simple, so much so that most of them come with no user manual. Even traditional non-technology users such as children, homemakers, and senior citizens across the globe, enjoy them and find them easy to operate. Apple believes in a reductionist approach to product design—remove all the clutter and make it easy for people to use the products.

Rams captures not just design but the whole world in these ten principles. Some people might argue they are more applicable for a world with physical products, but I think they are equally applicable for a digital world because they relate to a formless notion of design as a philosophy rather than any specific technology, methods, or practices.

So, how we do bring these ideas into our software products?

---

[24]"None of the World's Top Industries Would Be Profitable If They Paid for the Natural Capital They Use," http://grist.org/business-technology/none-of-the-worlds-top-industries-would-be-profitable-if-they-paid-for-the-natural-capital-they-use/

Human-Centered Design

When it comes to software products, designers got a rather late start. Our initial products were meant for people like us—techies. Consequently, it was not very uncommon for us techies to actually design our products. Pretty much throughout the 1990s in several global products companies where I worked we never had a specialist user experience designer on our teams, and software engineers would draw up wireframes and build mock-ups. In many cases, we even created the "UI Style Guide" that would specify a product's look and feel, its appearance, its interaction design, and so on. As a matter of fact, most of us were computer science graduates with no knowledge of something as basic as color theory, let alone the ability to understand the complexities of creating a "wow" experience. As a result, our products were reasonably high on technology and extremely low on user experience.

In the late 80s and early 90s, IBM started the PC revolution and filled up every office and eventually every home with one such machine. For the first time, we had users who were more "regular" humans—school kids, senior citizens, homemakers, non-PhDs, and so on. They were not technologically savvy to begin with and sought comfort in simplicity as they did with other day-to-day products. Microsoft Windows operating system did manage to fill that void at the OS level, even though we were not really thinking hard about building products with real humans in mind.

Starting with the iPod, and then the iPhone and iPad, Apple broke new ground by placing a device in each pocket. It threatens to disrupt the market once again by putting another device on every wrist. What IBM did to homes and offices, Apple did to every user—created a personal computing device that hardly looked like a traditional computer. It looked cute, required no extra-terrestrial intelligence to operate, and worked! It resonated deeply with the users for whom it was designed. As a result, Apple has become that iconic company that now commands 92% of the entire smartphone industry's profits even though it only sells 20% of its products.[25] It looks even more remarkable when you realize there are over 1,000 makers of smartphones and Apple is the undisputed king by many, many billions of dollars.

So, what did Apple do differently that several others couldn't? It was on the verge of bankruptcy in 1997 and was ironically bailed out by archrival Microsoft's investment. However, that only provided badly needed funds. What else did it do? Its focus on design or, more specifically, human-centered design led to such unprecedented success.

---

[25]"Apple's Share of Smartphone Industry's Profits Soars to 92%," www.wsj.com/articles/apples-share-of-smartphone-industrys-profits-soars-to-92-1436727458

Stated simply, human-centered design is a mindset that recognizes we can build better products by learning from our users. It seeks to learn about people for whom it is designing, understand their pain points, get their feedback on an early and frequent basis, and eventually deliver them just what they need. This is a major contrast with the hitherto technology-led design that sought to deliver top-end technology irrespective of whether it made sense to users. It is more like designing a product or a system with an outside-in perspective.

Apart from the mindset, there are human-centered design methods and techniques that help us understand aspects of "real human" users. Let's explore some of them.

User Personas

Consider the Swiss Army Knife. Originally designed as military ware, it is an ideal tool for someone who goes out hiking in the woods. It helps with four or five of the most common needs of someone trekking or camping. Now imagine we have the following conversation with some non-customers of the Swiss Army Knife:

> "This is so cool, but I would like it to have a laser pointer to help point to a location at night. As a camp guide, that would help me keep my team focused, especially on a dark night."

> "I am a writer, and I wish they had a pen in it—I always forget to carry one."

> "It would be so nice to have a solar charger for my smartphone. I love to take calls with my clients when outdoors, and I don't want to be stuck with a dead phone."

Now imagine we decide to include these three customer types in the profile of our target product users. To do so, we need to include their requirements so they feel interested in our product. The result might be a bloated mega knife that is so bulky to carry, it upsets everyone because it tries to please them all at the same time!

So, how do we decide whom to build it for? There might be several customer segments or customer types with varying interest levels (which would accordingly impact the business potential). Accommodating them all sure seems like a recipe for disaster. On the other hand, if we have to pick up a few of them, whom do we pick first, and, eventually, how do we address the rest of them, if we must address them all?

That's where user personas come in handy. Cooper first proposed the concept of user personas in *The Inmates Are Running the Asylum*. In a blog post on the origin of personas,[26] he refers to some of his earlier work in 1995 when he became so frustrated talking to developers that he eventually demanded to speak to customers instead. While talking to customers, he was able to draw out their commonalities and think of them in terms of their goals, tasks, and skill levels. When he used these hypothetical archetypes, he felt the developers could relate to them much better. Cooper's work led to the so-called goal-directed design methodology.[27]

Personas are the customer archetypes that allow us to focus on the primary user of a product. This aligns extremely well with the agile way of thinking by focusing on the highest-value requirements for the most important customers and gradually evolving the product over time to address a secondary persona. It is also possible that a business might decide to only focus on a primary persona just to retain the sharp focus of the product. Nonetheless, personas are a great tool to get a deeper understanding of the target customers, and a typical persona definition captures critical demographical and ethnographical information about it. The typical building blocks of a person include the following:

- Profile
- Personality
- Referents and Influences
- Archetypes and Quotes
- Technology Expertize
- User Experience Goals
- Used Device and Platforms
- Domain Details
- Must Do, Must Never
- Brand and Product Relationship

Again, there is no standard template for personas—the business must consider the most critical elements relevant to their market, customers, and products, and then construct the personas.

---

[26]"The Origin of Personas," www.cooper.com/journal/2003/08/the_origin_of_personas
[27]"Inside Goal-Directed Design: A Two-Part Conversation with Alan Cooper," www.cooper.com/journal/2014/04/inside-goal-directed-design-a-two-part-conversation-with-alan-cooper

The process of creating personas involves significant commitments of time, effort, and money. It often takes up to six months to come up with personas. If you don't have that much time, brainstorming is a shortcut you can use to come up with what is known as a "proto-persona." A proto-persona offers limited insight, rather "guesstimates," into customer archetypes without actually talking to them and, thus, could have serious limitations on its real utility. However, creating a proto-persona does have advantages—it just doesn't have the accuracy of user research and might have a bunch of untested hypotheses. So, while brainstorming might be a great starting point, especially in the absence of anything better, it is important to test your assumptions in the field rather than invest time and money to build a product based simply on those meeting-room assumptions.

Empathy Map

While a user persona might give you a broad picture of who your (target) customers are and what they "look" like, that information alone might not be adequate to learn how they find doing business with you. Why do they want your product, and what do they think or feel when using your product?

Often, we don't fully understand these questions because, as product developers, we have a limited interaction with our real users. A quantitative market survey could bring hard numbers that don't tell much about customers' motivation, frustrations, and so on.

An empathy map[28] is a simple way to visually capture such "sensory" information about your users. Originally created by Dave Gray of XPLANE, its goal is to "gain a deeper level of understanding of a stakeholder in your business ecosystem, which may be a client, prospect, partner, etc., within a given context, such as a buying decision or an experience using a product or service."[29] This is especially helpful when you can create a typical empathy map in something as frugal as a 20-minute workshop.

While creating a user persona is one technique to learn from a large number of target customers about their pain points, we don't quite have the product or service in mind. The user personas, as useful as they are, could still appear like "lifeless" categorizations without a real sense of how they will respond to a given product or service. An empathy map could give additional insights from the target customers on how they think or feel about a specific problem or a solution, and it could be an extremely rapid way to collect insights to get the rest of work started.

---

[28]"Empathy Map," http://gamestorming.com/core-games/empathy-mapping/
[29]"Empathy Map—Dave Gray," http://gamestorming.com/core-games/empathy-mapping/

Customer Journey Map

Let's say you are in the business of supplying made-to-order cakes. Your customers contact you via phone calls, e-mails, mobile apps, or chats and place their order for either standard items in your catalog or make customized orders. You might build the back-end infrastructure to effectively address your requirements to front-end with the customer's buying process.

However, do you know how they find doing business with you? What pain points do they face in finding you, choosing the right products, or placing the order and checking out? It is likely in some cases that your product makes life difficult for them. How do you discover these insights and capture them in an actionable manner?

A customer journey map could be a helpful visualization of the user experiences across the whole buying process. Adaptive Path[30] defines it "as a strategic process of capturing and communicating complex customer interactions. The activity of mapping builds knowledge and consensus across your organization, and the map helps build seamless customer experiences." It further describes the four steps of experience mapping:

- **Uncover the truth:** Sometimes we work with several pre-conceived notions or one-sided assumptions about the way users like to use a given product or service. Unless we make efforts to really observe their usage habits and learn about their experiences, we might not be able to uncover the truth.

- **Chart the course:** Quite often, we tend to simply pick up individual touch points without fully understanding the end-to-end journey that might give far better and actionable insights. Charting the entire course could help us understand if there are interdependencies in various steps, or if there are individual outliers that create disengagement despite an otherwise wow experience.

- **Tell the story:** While having raw data and insights is great, what really engages the audience is a story that brings out its finer points in rich details and provides an emotional connection. When the storytelling involves lifelike characters, we develop a much higher sense of empathy, which is a great first step in design thinking as well.

---

[30]Adaptive Path Mapping Experiences - http://mappingexperiences.com/

- **Use the map:** The map is not just a way to make notes from a field trip, but it must provide actionable insights that allow a team to work on specific pain points in the journey. Most importantly, it allows everyone on the team to have a single shared vision of the customer journey and not everyone's individual guesses and interpretations of what the problem might be.

There are several ways to describe an experience map, but the basic framework is a timeline that describes how a customer interacts with the system through its various touch points. It identifies their experiences (positive or negative) on a graded scale.

You could typically organize a workshop to learn from your customers and document an experience map. The whole aspect of customer collaboration, teamwork, and visual thinking makes an extremely valuable tool to understand our customers better in order to develop products and services with a better user experience.

Lean UX

Jeff Gothelf and Josh Seiden's 2013 book *Lean UX: Applying Lean Principles to Improve User Experience* was one of the earliest discussions on this subject. They mashed up lean (startups), design thinking and agile development as the foundations that influence lean UX.

In their book, they identified the following principles of lean UX:

- Cross-functional teams
- Small, dedicated, co-located
- Progress = outcomes, not output
- Problem-focused teams
- Removing waste
- Small batch size
- Continuous discovery
- GOOB[31]: The new user-centricity
- Shared understanding
- Anti-pattern: Rockstars, gurus, and ninjas
- Externalizing your work

---

[31]Steve Blank's famous mantra for all entrepreneurs" "Get out of the building."

- Making over analysis
- Learning over growth
- Permission to fail
- Getting out of the deliverables business

With the foundations of lean UX (lean, design thinking and agile development), most of these ideas reinforce each other and help build small, cross-functional teams that focus on delivering business-driven values and outcomes in an iterative manner. These ideas are especially potent in solving the "unknown-unknown" class of problems where there can't possibly be any previously known patterns of success. Surely, there are principles that guide the team to behave in some specific manner. The tools that the teams use are rather the same in terms of its "atomic operations," but the way they are applied or the sequence in which they are applied is highly fluid, iterative, and indeterministic. However, an empowered team of experts will invariably find its way to accomplish the desired results by sticking to these fundamental principles.

Figure 5-1 illustrates the lean UX process.

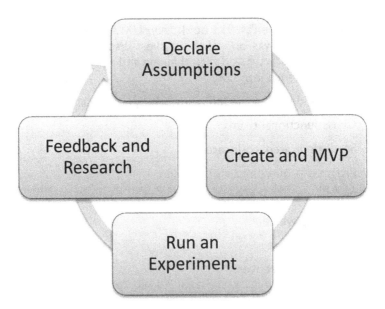

Figure 5-1. The lean UX process

Declaring assumptions is a critical starting point that allows the team to focus on outcomes rather than on a specific output to be delivered. In a lean startup fashion, we treat requirements as hypotheses. However, it might be too costly to build the entire product just to validate those hypotheses—perhaps the whole point of validation becomes moot if we have to build the entire system! So, lean UX talks about identifying the riskiest assumptions and creating a minimum viable product (MVP) that could be built quickly and cheaply and could offer decisive data points around the riskiest hypotheses through a series of experiments. Many such experiments might have very short run, again in order to optimize the total time through the learning loop, and they might use techniques such as A/B testing or a multivariate testing. Finally, these tests result in lots of data that serves as feedback to further improve the idea. The entire process goes on until the team has verified that its assumptions have been rigorously tested. Now it is all about implementing (or developing) the feature as a properly designed and well-tested software.

A key point about lean UX is that it is not a one-off activity only meant to be undertaken at the start of a product development endeavor. Rather, it is best served in small doses in each sprint of the agile development cycle. This avoids the risk of a big-bang disruption as well as the pitfall of going on without user feedback for far too long and risking the upfront design and development efforts. When lean UX practices are undertaken in an agile methodology such as scrum, they are performed inside the stories picked up for each of the sprints.

What about Software Design?

Software design is all about how the software accomplishes its intended functionality. Software design is the inner core of how components of software interact with each other and how the overall system eventually interacts with the external world. If that is not well designed, no amount of shiny wrapping can help.

Paul Ralph's PhD guide, Yair Wand, asked him to clearly define what we mean by (software) design. Together they came up with the following definition[32]:

> DESIGN: (noun) a specification of an object, manifested by some agent, intended to accomplish goals, in a particular environment, using a set of primitive components, satisfying a set of requirements, subject to some constraints.

Every decision or action pertaining to software design can perhaps be summed up in this definition. However, how we carry out that definition is more relevant to this book.

In the traditional waterfall world, software was designed in the so-called Big Design Up Front[33] (BDUF) manner—an approach that seeks to nail down and document every single detail before starting to write code. The approach

---

[32]"Is There a Scientific Definition of 'Design'?," www.fastcodesign.com/1672937/is-there-a-scientific-definition-of-design
[33]"Big Design Up Front," https://en.wikipedia.org/wiki/Big_Design_Up_Front

compartmentalizes design from its subsequent stage of construction (or actually writing the software). While this might have been an acceptable, or even a good strategy in the past, it relies on documentation as a source of validating the correctness of program logic. This practice is questionable today, given that it is far cheaper, faster, and effective to simply write software and test the program logic and correctness than to first write about it in documents, review it, and then finally implement it. Also, the decision to specify all details upfront (even if possible) can only make later-day changes harder to achieve. Martin Fowler in his highly influential 2004 blog post "Is Design Dead?,"[34] refers to the inadequacy of a planned software approach that is all about putting together the big building blocks, or designing the software, as being distinct from writing it.

Agile paradigm places lower importance on the traditional BDUF. It places a much higher importance on the evolutionary/emergent design (also known as continuous design). It was popularized by proponents of extreme programming, and it seeks to "reduce time to market for agile teams by incrementally formulating the design while implementing the software."[35] Rigorous self-testing software and design steps undertaken in short quantum throughout the lifecycle often accompany it.

However, many software developers consider the concepts of agility and architecture to be antithetical. Traditionally, architecture design has been considered the heavy-lifting activity that creates a robust architecture—something that might require a more rigorous and prolonged process than what could be possibly accomplished in, say, a two-week iteration. As a result, the agile way of architecture design is often seen as a very "soft" approach. I often meet engineers from systems companies or finance companies who consider their software to be "extremely complex"—and not like a "cute-looking" web site! However, I believe they are taking a narrow view of architecture design.

A key difference between traditional architecture design and agile architecture design is that architecture design happens throughout the lifecycle. As a result, we are not only incrementally evolving it, we are also constantly validating it. As a practice, a team might still perform a high-level architecture design at the start of the project based on the details known to it, but might stop short of getting into operational details knowing that the nature of software requirements is "emergent." In addition, with increasing clarity about the problem domain, we will also evolve the solution. In terms of implementing it,

---

[34]"Is Design Dead?," http://martinfowler.com/articles/designDead.html
[35]"Practice: Evolutionary Design," http://epf.eclipse.org/wikis/openup/practice.tech.evolutionary_design.base/guidances/practices/evolutionary_design_DE27D8D9.html

the code is typically created using agile engineering practices—such as test-driven development and refactoring—and integrated using practices such as continuous integration, which allows validating the design. Collectively, these practices help build software incrementally, test it continuously, and adapt it gracefully in short durations, sometimes as small as 20 or 30 minutes, throughout the time a product is being actively worked upon. As a result, while the heavy lifting might be missing from the process, the architecture of the product gets constantly validated iteratively and incrementally, and built in an extremely robust manner.

Unlike traditional architecture design that was often documented in Word documents, agile favors creating working software to specify or document it. Of course, as needed, other artifacts such as UML, event-trace diagrams, and the class hierarchy diagrams might still be created, but a well-documented and self-testing code is perhaps far more effective to "describe" the architecture design. Among other things, it helps eliminate the need for paper reviews by creating a working software that can be executed and tested to validate the architecture.

Software architecture and design is a key pillar of software construction. The knowledge and skills required are often specialized and though agile methods (specifically Scrum, where there is no such role of an "architect") tend to democratize it. I don't believe everyone on the team can simply perform these activities—most certainly not on day one of the project!

At an individual level, one could surely accomplish lower-level design, say, of a private method, or how a particular database search query is written to minimize the query time, but at a systems level, it typically entails high-level considerations of system performance and scale, among others. As opposed to the waterfall model, agile thinking aims to validate the key assumptions before getting to the next levels of details, but at every point, creating assets and artifacts that can be quickly executed to validate its underlying assumptions.

At a high level, agile methods recognize the need for defining such system architecture albeit not in a highly detailed manner, while at a low level, the thinking is to implement design in code using agile engineering methods such as TDD, refactoring and CI. These methods allow the design to be constantly tested and corrected, building in the quality and keeping a check on the so-called technical debt lest a great design eventually becomes unusable due to subsequent haphazard changes that never get properly tested or adequately refactored.

In the overall context of product development using agile methodologies, the fundamental techniques or practices around software architecture and design need to be practiced in short feedback loops. They also need to operate under a large umbrella of the overall architecture. The technical architecture thus evolves based on how the system gets incrementally developed and constantly tested in the real world.

Conclusion

Great design is simple and puts users in direct control of their products and services. It establishes the emotional connection that causes consumers to buy a product or service they crave (sometimes even at a higher price point than its competitors) and ultimately creates a "stickiness."

However, design is not simply about having a slick UI or window dressing a bad product! While visual design is an important and integral element of the overall design process, a successful product engages its users with an overall user experience that might span from the time they decide to research a product to the time they purchase it and start using it. In fact, other aspects of design only begin to be visible when the users start using the product, whereas "user experience" is a much more broad and pervasive term.

Despite the foundation of some of the timeless principles that the subject of design stands firmly on, technology is a big driver of how it is actually implemented. Thirty or forty years ago, we had monochrome displays with poor resolution. It was more common to have command-line interfaces (CLI) than graphical user interfaces (GUI). Over time, the GUI technology has invaded our space to the point that they are not just limited to computers but have been adopted to watches, phones, cameras, and so on. However, the coming future might once again disrupt that all!

Aaron Shapiro, author of an interesting article on anticipatory design, "The Next Big Thing in Design? Less Choice,"[36] argues the case for simplifying design (and choices) even further. As opposed to current trends where the designer does the "thinking" on behalf of the user, she might be responsible for creating a platform or service that rather "anticipates" the next logical move of a user and takes action automatically. For example, the system might learn that the user is on his way home and knows from past experience that it will take ten minutes to brew the coffee. The designer would consider these factors and adjust the system accordingly.

The coming age of the Internet of Things (IoT) promises 50 billion interconnected devices in just the next five years. That's an impressive seven devices per human being! However, not all devices will perhaps have user interfaces as we take for granted today. Indeed, a majority of them might have "Zero UI"— and in its simplest form, there might not be a "screen" as we take know it today.

---

[36]www.fastcodesign.com/3045039/the-next-big-thing-in-design-fewer-choices

Its most complex forms could include motion-controlled, touch interfaces, voice-controlled or thought-reading cognitive computing. In any case, this is a major paradigm shift on product design. Many of the mental models will likely be disrupted, and apart from the quintessential visual design, we might soon be exploring new elements of design. As Andy Goodman remarked,[37] we might become the next UI!

---

[37]"What is Zero UI? (And Why It Is Crucial to the Future Of Design)," John Brownlee, www.fastcodesign.com/3048139/what-is-zero-ui-and-why-is-it-crucial-to-the-future-of-design

Develop

Let's do it!

Ready, fire, aim: the fast approach to software development. Ready, aim, aim, aim, aim: the slow approach to software development.

—Author unknown[1]

We all come up with lots of ideas every day despite varying levels of intelligence, experience, and exposure. Some people believe we might generate tens of thousands of ideas on a daily basis.[2] While most ideas are fun to think about (imagine if we could move things by mere thoughts or if champagne flowed in municipal taps, just like water!), they are usually too impractical, obscure, wild, or outrageous to follow up on. Only a small percentage of ideas are actually worth pursuing.

However, many ideas become valuable when we take them out of our heads and start turning them into something tangible—be it a wooden bench, an origami bird, a house made of LEGOs, or a few lines of software code. In most cases, one needs to have a few basic resources to perform some experiments with ideas. We generally lack either the skills or resources to bring our ideas to life, or we are too afraid of peer ridicule or social rejection. Hence, our ideas die an unnatural death before they are given a fair chance.

Fortunately, the software industry is blessed with an amazing medium that allows developing ideas into a tangible experiment with a rather small investment of time, effort, and money. If the experiment works as promised, one

[1] www.quotegarden.com/programming.html
[2] "The 70,000 Thoughts Per Day Myth?" Neuroskeptic, http://blogs.discovermagazine.com/neuroskeptic/2012/05/09/the-70000-thoughts-per-day-myth/

could then decide to build it as a full-fledged product. Many people consider the process of development the soul of software development. Indeed, being able to develop something of value is a source of great joy!

However, in reality, software development doesn't always go so smoothly. It has traditionally been plagued with delays, cost overruns, poor quality, and people issues. Starting with the critique of the waterfall model by Winston Royce in his famous 1970 paper "Managing the Development of Large Software Systems,"[3] enough anecdotal data exists to prove that waterfall simply isn't the right approach for software development. Strangely, our industry still loves waterfall because it seems to provide a sense of safety. In most cases, we simply pad estimates that give both a false sense of accuracy and precision at the same time. Since it is better than living with a sense of uncertainty, we prefer it. Customers are happy because they have an ironclad guarantee that they will receive the software by the deadline. The suppliers are happy because they have contained the requirements in a base-lined document and have padded the budget enough to make money even in the worst-case scenario. And the engineers have no option but to accept whatever work there is to do. Project managers are assigned to execute and are perhaps the most hassled of all—we blame delays on poor execution because we believe that's the only thing that could lead to the grounding of the project when everything else is so clear. The teams create reams of documentation and send useless status reports to keep the hope of a software shipment alive. In the end, teams work hundred-hour weeks and somehow ship a buggy product without several key features, while the lawyers on both sides argue who was wrong in specifying or understanding the requirements. The vendors hope the customers will have no option but to trigger the change management process to handle additional requirements. This game is played every time—just the setting differs. Sadly, no one seemed to mind it for a long time. Thankfully, businesses today are being held accountable for such inglorious mismanagement.

Our challenge today is to develop better products faster and cheaper. How do we leverage the continuous feedback work cycle, and how do we ensure the highest-value delivery with every increment?

In this chapter, we shall study various agile methods used to develop software products.

---

[3]"Managing the Development of Large Software Systems," Dr. Winston Royce, www.serena.com/docs/agile/papers/Managing-The-Development-of-Large-Software-Systems.pdf

The World Before

Until the 90s, we used a simplistic model of software development that was essentially wrong. In this so-called waterfall method, we essentially "captured" 100% of the requirements upfront (Big Requirements Up Front, or "BRUF") and designed the entire system (Big Design Up Front, or "BDUF") before getting on with strictly sequential downstream phases of implementation, coding, and testing. Once the coding phase was completed, the teams would start a big-bang integration phase and, upon its completion, start the testing phase.

Even though this model seemed like a fairly logical process for developing software, it was conceptually wrong and technically ineffective on multiple counts, but largely due to one key reason—that we took what was essentially a production model in the manufacturing industry and applied it to what is essentially a design problem in the software world of knowledge creation. In production, we must clearly understand the process steps, and we must be able to replicate them one after other in a pre-specified sequence to get the pre-determined output. If we have the right raw material at every pre-specified phase and its quality is of acceptable level, we are (almost) guaranteed to get the final product out by following all steps of the process. If there are problems with the product in its intermediate or final stages, we can apply quality-assurance and quality-control principles. Since we are going to run this process hundreds and thousands of times, we can additionally apply principles of statistical process control (SPC) and tools such as Six Sigma to systemically eliminate or minimize normal variations and improve the quality of an existing product.

Take the case of Coke. For over a hundred years, Coke has manufactured its sugared beverage in most countries of the world. Even though its exact chemical formulation is supposedly a secret, its manufacturing process must be so crystal clear that it can be translated into any known language in any country where it can be carried out by the local bottlers. Now imagine being able to sustain this level of process rigor for over hundred years, and you will pretty soon recognize that this process isn't black magic and it doesn't rely on expert minds or skilled hands alone. It must be extremely transparent so that it can be followed consistently, and since it pertains to something consumable, it must also adhere to every country's food safety laws. The process must be repeatable so that it can be executed day in and day out without any loss in product quality, despite any variations in quality of raw materials, such as water, etc.. Finally, it must be scalable, which means it can be manufactured all over the world. (In other words, the process doesn't depend on any specific cultural way of doing things, and the raw materials, factory, and machinery are available or able to be constructed just about anywhere.)

Now contrast this with a knowledge creation work. Say that you are helping your eighth-grade daughter with project on solving nutrition problems for homeless people, or that you are a master chef trying to invent a new recipe for this year's New Year's party, or that you are a software engineer trying to find a new way for people to bank more easily on their smartphones. Do you know the process that will lead you to the final outcome? For that matter, do you even know what the final outcome is? If we go by the recent history of successful companies such as PayPal and Instagram, we find the final services were not the initial ideas. PayPal and Instagram started out as Confinity and Burbn, respectively, as their "Plan A," and they pivoted to their current avatars, which were more like their "Plan B" or "Plan C" as they learned more about the market. Sticking to a predetermined waterfall-ish plan would have only resulted in what I call an "operation successful, but the patient died" scenario. (Eric Ries calls it "achieving failure.")

So, clearly the manufacturing metaphor was not the right solution for modern-day, knowledge-intensive work such as software creation. Software development projects were beginning to go awry due to the wrong approach as early as the 60s. Frederick Brooks was the manager of the software team that built IBM/360, one of the most famous and successful operating systems. He had over 1,000 software engineers on his team in 1964–65. He learned a lot from that experience—so much that he ended up writing the 1975 software project management classic *The Mythical Man-Month*. In the book, Brooks identifies several issues leading to a software project's going awry:

- Techniques of estimating are poorly developed.
- Estimating techniques fallaciously confuse effort with progress.
- Because we are uncertain of estimates, we are not able to forecast accurately.
- Schedule progress is poorly monitored.
- Manpower is added to a late project.

Unfortunately, there was no real alternative to the then prevalent methods, even though practitioners like Harlan Mills were beginning to experiment with incremental methods. As a result, not much changed throughout the 70s and the 80s.

In 1986, Brooks postulated the famous "No Silver Bullet" (NSB) argument: "There is no single development, in either technology or management technique, which by itself promises even one order-of-magnitude improvement within a decade in productivity, in reliability, in simplicity." Surely we have seen many such "silver bullets" in software industry since then. Brooks calls out ideas even during his time such as object-oriented programming, artificial intelligence, expert systems, "automatic" programming, graphical programming, program verification, environment and tools, workstations, and so on. The NSB theory proved provocative and in the 1995 edition of his book, Brooks discussed the impact on quality and productivity, asserting that, despite authors of respective methodologies claiming a ten-fold improvement as a result of their methodologies, the reality was otherwise.

Does it mean we are doomed with the status quo?

Thankfully, software thinkers and leading practitioners continued experimenting with ways to improve software development methods.

Extreme Programming

One effort that gained popularity was Kent Beck's C3 project at Chrysler Corporation in the late 90s. It advocated rapid cycles of software creation followed by periodic feedback. Unlike the slow-moving, long cycle of quintessential document-driven and hand-offs-led development and post-facto feedback of yesteryears, it was considered "extreme" and focused on delivering the software (that is, programming). Hence, the moniker "Extreme Programming" stuck. Extreme Programming, or simply XP, was a set of principles and practices that Beck brought to the sinking C3 payroll project, managing to bring it out of chaos, though not before it was eventually killed. What Kent brought to the table was radical ideas to the software engineering world, but were reasonably well proven in other industries. For example, NASA had reported test-first development much earlier in the 60s. As I also discussed in earlier chapters, Kelly's Skunk Works also pioneered several ideas that resemble modern-day XP predecessors, at least as far as new product development is concerned. The original idea of a 40-hour workweek ironically came from Henry Ford[4] in a manufacturing environment in the early twentieth century. Ford recognized that human capability was beginning to be considered depletable and susceptible to errors unless adequately rested from time to time.

XP defined 12 core practices, "XpXtudes,"[5] that the XP programmers do, grouped into four categories:

- Fine-scale feedback

  - Test-driven development

  - Planning game

  - Whole team

  - Pair programming

---

[4]"Where Did the 40-Hour Workweek Come From?"
[5]"XPXtudes," http://c2.com/cgi/wiki?XpXtude

- Continuous process rather than batch
  - Continuous integration
  - Design improvement
  - Small releases
- Shared understanding
  - Simple design
  - System metaphor
  - Collective code ownership
  - Coding standard
- Programmer welfare
  - Sustainable pace

Today, XP as a methodology is all but dead, but its practices, especially the technical practices, are once again being recognized as a better way to bake in software quality as compared to an inspection-based approach. Some practices like coding standard were not really new, but simply gained more attention. Continuous integration was a new practice that eventually got elevated to continuous delivery and continuous deployment, and it has almost become table stakes in modern-day software development, even more so for online software. Other technical practices such as the test-driven development and code refactoring require strong technical and design skills, and they have not always been practiced by a majority of teams. However, there is a sense of belated recognition that ignoring XP practices and practicing Scrum with waterfall-era engineering practices was not the best way to achieve agility.

In addition to placing very high premium on such technical practices, XP also identified five core values:[6] communication, simplicity, feedback, respect, and courage. However, there is an invisible secret sauce of a team's sociology that binds it all together in a way that Jim Highsmith reflected in his 2001 interview with Kent[7]—the "social contracts." While most people today recognize XP's important contribution to technical practices, much of its key learning from its social context paved the way for the Agile Manifesto, which was essentially bereft of any technical practices. XP largely established agile as more of a "people" thing than a "process" thing.

---

[6]"Extreme Programming: A Gentle Introduction," www.extremeprogramming.org/
[7]"Interview with Kent Beck (circa 2001)," Jim Highsmith, https://dzone.com/articles/interview-kent-beck-circa-2001

Agile

During the 90s, multiple approaches were being experimented and improved upon by software practitioners. Some of them were the big daddies of process world, such as Software Engineering Institute's Capability Maturity Model (Software CMM, or CMMi as it is known currently) or the highly institutional ISO9000 (originally starting as ISO9000 TickIT). While these large standards and frameworks were created in response to the alarming percentage of failed and challenged projects, they were rather ill suited to an ever-changing world. Even today, a significant number of (mostly large) companies use these frameworks. For example, the number of companies that report using a CMMi framework continues to post a modest 10% year-on-year growth. However, it wouldn't be inaccurate to say that agile methods are now the mainstream way of software development, even though a typical adoption curve could be expected across industries.

Some of the other leading ideas that built upon foundational incremental and iterative methods have significantly contributed to the agile thinking in software development include (in no particular order of importance): Tom Gilb's Evo, Alistair Cockburn's Crystal Clear, Dynamic Systems Development (DSDM), Jeff De Luca's Feature-Driven Development (FDD), Jim Highsmith's Adaptive Software Development (ASD), and so on. In most cases, the methods had more in common in terms of values and principles (even if they were not always explicitly articulated in that many words) and differed only a little on specific methods and practices. These similarities paved the way for significantly advancing the body of knowledge when 17 leading methodologists came together at a ski resort in Utah in 2001 and decided to put their ideas and thoughts in a blender and created the Agile Manifesto.

Agile Manifesto

As we discussed in Chapter 1, the Agile Manifesto was an important milestone in the history of software development, embracing some of the best ideas and thoughts of that time, in 2001. Since then, we have seen more initiatives to integrate agile thinking into product development and other aspects of businesses.

When I am training, I always put up an image of the Agile Manifesto and explain its four values (and twelve principles in the longer version of my training). No one has ever really questioned or disagreed on the utility or relevance of the Agile Manifesto, even in 2015. Clearly, these four lines continue to be critical to software development. Indeed, there have been many more such manifestos subsequently, including some by the original signatories of the Agile Manifesto themselves. For example, in today's world, a "working software" might not be simple enough—you might want to know how many people are actually using it? Or responding to change might simply demonstrate a follower's mindset, while the leader might actually be the disruptor, the risk-taker, or the harbinger, of change. Clearly, the Agile Manifesto seems to be an archeological remnant of time frozen in 2001. However, when my colleagues in consulting and coaching rightly point out that a significant majority of teams they work with still struggle to even get to that point, I am reminded that we will continue to see varying levels of maturities of software teams.

However, my advice to the uninitiated would be to closely examine the Agile Manifesto and embrace its purpose, values, and principles. When there is a better basis for breaking the mold, by all means go ahead and create your own agile manifesto that works for you better than the standard version.

The PM Declaration of Interdependence

In 2005, a few leading software community leaders came together (some of whom were the original signatories of the Agile Manifesto in 2001) and created the so-called "Declaration of Interdependence,"[8] or the DOI. The DOI specifically calls out the notion of "interdependence" being vital to the success of software development endeavors, which is a rather broad term that includes customers, stakeholders, teams, and so on.

The declaration goes like this:

Agile and adaptive approaches for linking people, projects, and value.

We are a community of project leaders that are highly successful at delivering results. To achieve these results:

- We **increase return on investment** by *making continuous flow of value our focus.*
- We **deliver reliable results** by *engaging customers in frequent interactions and shared ownership.*
- We **expect uncertainty** and *manage it through iterations, anticipation, and adaptation.*
- We **unleash creativity and innovation** by *recognizing that individuals are the ultimate source of value, and creating an environment where they can make a difference.*
- We **boost performance** through *group accountability for results and shared responsibility for team effectiveness.*
- We **improve effectiveness and reliability** through *situationally specific strategies, processes and practices.*

---

[8]"Declaration of Interdependence," http://pmdoi.org/

Among other things, the DOI also lays a strong foundation for agile project management, specifically by calling out the last value—we could be much more effective by being dynamically adaptive to the situation and to the needs of the projects and teams rather than following overly standardized and static processes.

I always view the declaration as a set of guiding principles for managing projects in an agile environment—something that the original Agile Manifesto didn't articulate in so many words. The specific process or the method is not so important, but being consciously aware of the values and principles allows a (thinking) practitioner to explore answers and find solutions without being directed to follow some prescription for every single conceivable situation. Even though there are specific frameworks, such as Scrum, that elaborate upon how some specific management practices are applied in real-world agile projects, I think a deep understanding of the core principles of the DOI go a long way in preparing an agile mindset that isn't always looking for applying a cookie-cutter solution to every problem, but is willing to explore every problem as unique by applying fundamental atomic operations that collectively help solve the problem more effectively. The real judgment is in knowing which of these atomic operations to be applied, in what degree, and when.

Scrum

The first mention of the word "Scrum" in software development came from Peter DeGrace and Leslie Hulet Stahl's 1991 software classic *Wicked Problems, Righteous Solutions: A Catalogue of Modern Engineering Paradigms*.

They drew inspiration from the famous 1986 HBR classic *The New New Product Development Game*[9] by Hirotaka Takeuchi and Ikujiro Nonaka, and wrote in Chapter 7 the "The All-at-Once Model":

> *If Scrum was applied to software development, it would go something like this:*
>
> *Suppose you have a software development project to do. For each traditional phase, you can draw from a pool of experienced people. Rather than have several designers do the design phase and have several coders do the construction phase, etc., you form a team by carefully selecting one person from each pool. During a team meeting, you will tell them that they have been carefully chosen to do a project that is very important to the company, country, organization, or whatever. This unsettles them*

---

[9]"The New New New Product Development Game," Hirotaka Takeuchi and Ikujiro Nonaka, https://hbr.org/1986/01/the-new-new-product-development-game

somewhat. You then give them a description of the problem to be solved, the figures for how much it cost in time and money to do similar projects, and what the performance figures for similar systems are. Then, after you have gotten them used to the idea that they are special, having been specially chosen and challenged to do an important job, you further unsettle the team by saying that their job is to produce the system in, say, half the time and money and it must have twice the performance of other systems. Next, you say that how they do it is their business. Your business is to support them in getting resources. Then, you leave them alone.

You stand by to give them advice if you are asked. You get their reports, which come regularly but not as often nor as voluminously as with the Waterfall. But, mostly you wait. In something like the appointed time, out pops the system with the performance and cost figures you wanted.

DeGrace and Stahl go on to describe just how an autonomous team, where members learn from and teach each other (by word of mouth), will self-organize in such an "all-at-once," or concurrent, engineering environment. On the need of management control, they further say:

To be sure, control is exercised; but, it is subtle and much of it is indirect. It is exercised by selecting the right people, creating an open work environment, encouraging feedback from the field, establishing an evaluation and reward system based on group performance, managing the tendency for going off in many directions early on and the need to integrate transformation and effort later on, tolerating and even anticipating mistakes, and encouraging suppliers to become involved early without controlling them.

I think they lay a solid foundation for agility with these words.

Jeff Sutherland and Ken Schwaber took the idea of Scrum into software development further[10] when they conceived the Scrum process in the early 90s[11], and presented "Scrum Software Development Process" at OOPSLA95.

Scrum process is founded on principles of empirical process control. It questions the ability and utility of making long-range predictions when there are several unknowns along the way. It seeks to minimize overall uncertainty and risk by initially saying no to the big upfront planning and instead developing slivers of completed functionality in short back-to-back timeboxes (known

---

[10]I haven't come across anything in Sutherland's or Schwaber's literature that suggests they either collaborated with DeGrace and Stahl, or referred to their book. However, I am only referring to the publication dates to refer to the timeline, and by no means implicating that these two ideas are the same or different

[11]"The History of Scrum," www.scrumguides.org/history.html

as "sprints") based on what we know right now (rather than what we might possibly need in the future) and prioritizing them per highest value, developing and delivering them iteratively and incrementally, and using the experience data to evolve the increasingly reliable long-range predictions about the release as we get better clarity later in the day. It seeks to keep its plans, work products, and progress (as well as impediments) transparent and highly visible to all stakeholders, including customers and team members alike, and practice a continuous "inspect-and-adapt" learning loop throughout the development cycle. Through such series of small in-process course corrections throughout the development, Scrum methodology seeks to maximize the chances of hitting the goals rather than hoping to accomplish them in the waterfall-style in one single, and rather questionable Hail Mary pass.[12]

The term "Scrum" denotes a cross-functional team, much like the Scrum formation in the game of rugby, where everyone in the team comes together and "holds the ball" and takes it to the other goalpost. Like in rugby, each player might have different skills and positions on the field. During a Scrum, they all might need to step out of their comfort zone and perform like a cross-functional team. Similarly, a software team might need to come out of its silo mindset and deliver the goods at the end of its sprint. This requires the team to own its process and self-organize itself according to the need of the moment. However, at an individual level, deep expertise might often become the impediment for someone trying to help his or her peers on the team. No one can plan for it on an emergency basis (which means the team must do what it can do best, given the situation), but teams could maximize their chances to deal with such anticipated scenarios in near-term future by continuously cross-training team members. Scrum calls this "generalizing specialists," and it is a very big part of building a culture of learning and growing Scrum teams and team members.

Scrum is often criticized for ignoring technical practices and making the entire framework appear so (deceptively) simple. In fact, the Scrum guide doesn't even mention practices such as test-driven development, refactoring, or continuous integration. Scrum is considered more of a framework than a process because it doesn't prescribe any specific technical practices. Such a "lightweight" approach has definitely helped make Scrum a popular choice in the industry across the globe, but it has also created significant problems. Since Scrum itself neither explicitly discourages such an approach nor actively promotes any specific way of "constructing" the software, most teams continue to blissfully implement waterfall-based linear phases and sequential engineering processes inside each sprint. The result is a "mini-waterfall" inside a sprint! While this by itself might or might not be a problem, it does limit the agility potential of the team, especially in a world where the cycle times are crashing

---

[12]"Hail Mary Pass," https://en.wikipedia.org/wiki/Hail_Mary_pass

with every passing day. With the advent of SaaS and mobile-based delivery models (which we discuss in Chapter 7), it is now almost every software's business to deliver to the customer's cadence. A mini-waterfall, on the other hand, might not only seriously limit a team's ability to "ship-at-will" but also make sprints very heavily backloaded and liable for rejection, especially by those seeking instant nirvana. This whole "Agile = Scrum" mindset has led to some serious damage to the agile movement, for it seems to eschew the very cause it was created to address—that is, focus on "individuals and interactions" more than on process and tools! Indeed, as part of my consulting practice, I see many organizations that felt shortchanged by Scrum and decided to discard it, sometimes even finding the comfort in good-old waterfall despite all its shortcomings!

Notwithstanding arguments for and against Scrum, it still is a great framework that helps build a management structure to deliver valuable software in short cadence. Given its huge adoption, there is also huge body of knowledge (and coaches, certifications, and trainers) to explain and describe its adoption.

The Scrum guide[13] remains the best concise presentation of the modern-day Scrum framework (which hasn't changed much since it was first announced and isn't likely to change much in the future[14]).

Lean

Henry Ford pioneered mass production of affordable cars. Over a period of 19 years starting in 1908, he was able to bring down the price of the famous Model T (also known as the "Tin Lizzie") from the initial introduction price of $950 to as little as $260[15] because he was able to mass-produce cars that were largely identical and employed interchangeable parts. This led to major economies of scale and created an extremely successful company for a country that was discovering its middle class in a growing economy. He sold over 15 million cars during that time, and at times, comprised as much as 40% of all the cars sold in the US market. However, the success of Ford was also its limitation. Ford's philosophy of offering standard design without any customization or personalization is summed up in these immortal words: "You can have any color of car as long as it is black." Ford offered only black cars between 1913 and 1925.

---

[13]"The Scrum Guide," www.scrumguides.org/scrum-guide.html
[14]Ken Schwaber, co-creator of Scrum, wrote in his 2007 book *The Enterprise and Scrum,* "There will be no Scrum Release 2.0 ... Why not? Because the point of Scrum is not to solve [specific problems of development] ... Scrum unearths the problems caused by the complexity and lets the organization solve them, one by one, over and over again"
[15]https://media.ford.com/content/fordmedia/fna/us/en/news/2013/08/05/model-t-facts.html

Ford pioneered an ultra-efficient production system where there was basically only one design of car that was mass-produced against market forecast and sold at a dealership. Having squeezed a great deal of efficiency from car-making innovations, Ford was rolling in lots of money. When the first Model T was introduced in 1908, Ford's profit margin was $220 per car. By 1914, it had dropped to $99. However, Ford was not worried about it. He was able to make cars cheaper by mass-producing them, and by passing on the cost savings to customers, he was able to make them even cheaper for more and more customers to afford them.

When Kiichoro Toyoda, son of Toyota Group founder Sakichi Toyoda first went to the US and Europe in 1929, he came back with lots of ideas to set up automobile production operations in Japan. However, his biggest challenge was to create a production system for the smaller market that Japan was. He recognized that unlike the US, he did not have the luxury of large volumes to accrue economies of scale. He was also interested in offering variability in design to the customers. Through a series of innovations, along with tremendous contributions from Taiichi Ohno, who was inspired by the efficient supermarkets in US, Toyota was able to create a system that did not offer any car on a cash-down basis! The customers could browse through the brochures, and maybe even check out a demo car or two, and select the car they wanted to buy. They would pay upfront for the car, and Toyota would only then start the production of the car using the so-called "pull production" method. Pull production allowed Toyota to maintain a minimum inventory of car parts in various stages of assembly (a zero inventory would have been technically the leanest operations but would have led to unacceptable delivery times, and hence a balance between inventory and delivery times was needed). During the production, Toyota would employ a series of simple but extremely powerful ideas to create a highly efficient system:

- **Just-in-time:** Rather than producing all the parts first and storing them for future use, and then transporting them when actually required, Toyota created a system for just-in-time production where production and subsequent transport would happen simultaneously, thereby significantly reducing the need for hand-offs and storage and transportation time and effort. This would be accomplished by a simple concept that would be intricately interconnected with all components, known as the "pull system."

- **Pull system/Kanban:** Unlike the conventional car making where the production was more like "push system," that is, the order fulfillment would start upstream irrespective of whether the downstream stations had available capacity to cope with the amount of flow or not. This would ensure that only the parts needed would be produced at the right time and in the right quantity. Toyota used a rather simple visual signaling mechanism to communicate a "pull" from downstream to upstream—a visual indicator card known as kanban would be moved and would indicate to the most immediate upstream process that a component created by it had been consumed, and that it must now replenish to maintain the stable number of semi-finished components at that level. That process would trigger similar kanbans to other feeding processes upstream and acquire components for it to assemble its own parts, and so on. The entire system would create only and exactly the number of parts that were needed by the actual customer demand that had been pulled by the most downstream process. In a steady state, the process is extremely effective in reducing the inventory at each stage without sacrificing the overall lead times.

- **Andon cord:** When a worker detects an issue, he is empowered to pull a cord passing overhead at all stations that will immediately bring the production of the entire line to a halt. This will attract everyone's attention to solve the problem, for if the issue is allowed to go uncorrected, it might create similar problems in all subsequent parts. The system requires empowering each worker with the judgment that he is trusted to make the right decision on behalf of the company—a very big deal, given the inordinate costs of halting the production line in any factory.

- **Single-piece flow:** In a traditional production set-up, the work planners might decide to fill up a large batch size to ensure high utilization of the costly machinery. However, if there is no firm demand for those items, the production might happen economically, but the surplus items of the batch will continue to be stored as inventory without any market demand, and eventually contribute to the waste. On the other hand, if we wait for the real demand to be available until the entire batch is filled up, we might lose on the customer lead time. Both the scenarios are bad. In lean, the production is done only against actual demand, and the idea is to reduce the batch size to as low as possible—ideally a single piece—so that one work piece is moved from one step to the next without waiting for the machine utilization. The idea is to have no work-in-progress, and thus eliminate inventories and create a single-piece flow in the shortest amount of time. It is also known as continuous flow. In addition to keeping the inventories low, the process is faster as the batch sizes are reduced, thus leading to reduced wait times at each of the interim workstations. Another positive side effect is to assess the quality of the finished piece and, if there are any issues, ensure that the system is immediately corrected so that similar defects don't recur.

- **Single-minute-exchange-of-dye:** A production setup could either have dedicated specialized machines for each specific operation or a process, or some generic machines that could be configured for multiple purposes. However, such reconfigurations normally take a lot of time and effort in changing over, thus literally offsetting any potential costs savings due to having lesser number of machines in a factory. When Toyota recognized that having specialized machines would also mean acquiring additional land (which was too costly in Japan) not just for the factory but also for keeping the vehicles for transportation, they started looking for opportunities to reduce the changeover/setup times. Shigeo Shingo created the SMED approach, which led over to a 40-fold improvement between 1975 and 1985.

Lean thinking was a major guiding force behind agile thinking, even though they have a subtle difference. While lean is all about reducing wastes from the system and thereby delivering the product faster and cheaper, agile is all about responding to changes faster. However, despite this subtle difference, there two share a fundamental philosophy and values even though specific methods might vary. Both talk about reducing batch sizes, creating single-piece flow, and implementing the notion of swarming in XP from the concept of the andon cord.

The ideas behind lean production were still largely considered unsuitable for software development, because of the fundamental differences between production and design. However, in 2003, Mary Poppendieck formally brought Lean thinking into software development when she wrote the book on "Lean

Software Development." Rather than giving another methodology or a process lifecycle, she proposed a set of practices that help reduce waste from the software development value stream. She identified the following principles of lean software development:[16]

- **Optimize the whole:** The strength of a chain is known by its weakest link, not the strongest link. In a value-creation process such as software development, if we continue optimizing the performance of a single step inside it, we might still be limited in terms of the overall performance by relatively weaker processes in rest of the process. Thus, lean promotes optimizing the whole rather than focusing only on parts. For example, it might not be enough to only focus on improving the unit testing if there are other serious issues in design.

- **Focus on customers:** Software development is a business-critical activity that must satisfy customer needs to be deemed useful. It is often very easy for development teams to lose track of customers and think of solutions in technical terms, resulting in bad product that either no one wants or requires too much of rework. We must be able to ask the right questions to understand customer needs better, which in turn helps us focus on solving the right problems, thereby leading to a great customer experience.

- **Energize workers:** The most precious resource for any enterprise, and more so for a software organization, is its people. If we don't have talented people who are seriously fired up by meaningful challenges and have been empowered to come up with creative ideas and solutions, we might soon lose their interest, energy, and engagement. Lean doesn't just stop at optimizing systems, but considers people as the most important aspect of problem-solving.

---

[16]"The Lean Mindset," http://poppendieck.com/

- **Eliminate waste:** In line with the original seven wastes identified in lean, Poppendieck identified equivalent wastes in software development:

  - **Partially done work:** Any partially done work adds up to unnecessary inventory that leads to no economic output of the process without answering the fundamental question. So, documentation or a piece of software that only addresses a part of the hypothesis might represent waste that must be avoided.

  - **Extra processes:** Poppendieck is extremely critical of "paperwork" that leads to the extra processes without adding to real customer value. She encourages exploration of better means to transmit or share information to reduce or eliminate any extra processing step.

  - **Extra features:** There is enough industry and anecdotal data to show that the majority of features in a software rarely or never get used. However, we spend a significant amount of effort and time to specify, design, implement, and test them all.

  - **Task switching:** Multitasking gives the impression that all the work streams are being served, but there are invisible costs of task switching that gradually add up to the overall lead times.

  - **Waiting:** A significant part of software development lead time is consumed by delays that lead to the downstream work waiting. The delays might be due to an extraordinary amount of documentation, reviews, decision, approvals, testing, deployment, and so on. A process where there are multiple hand-offs is especially prone to such delays and subsequent wait times.

- **Motion:** While in manufacturing it is easy to visualize the notion of unnecessary motion that could lead to wastes, in software development, motion is all about how much human effort or interaction it takes for a developer to find out given information. It also relates to a document being circulated among various groups so that information can be collated into it.

- **Defects:** As in manufacturing, any defects in software development are a source of customer dissatisfaction and will eventually need rework in order to fix them. The longer the defect stays in production, the more costly it might be to fix it.

- **Enhance Learning:** Unlike in production where the entire knowledge has to be mapped to a process before starting a production run, software development is more like a design activity where much of the knowledge will be discovered and created—and indeed, even discarded— before the final product is built. A software developer, therefore, must identify ways to enhance the learning by undertaking short experiments that allow for rapid validation of hypotheses, eliminating sources of variability, and using feedback to amplify learnings.

- **Increase flow:** Conventional economics of production emphasizes resource utilization, which could lead to surplus inventory that wipes out any short-term gains from mass production while reducing the speed of throughput. The software equivalent would be to execute software development in phases that aim to accomplish design or coding for all features. Lean software development favors creating a smooth flow, improving efficiency, and delivering value.

- **Build quality in:** The fundamental idea is to bake in the quality, that is, to find and fix defects closest to the origin of defects, before moving on to the next level of elaboration. This reduces the costly rework cycles downstream while also establishing predictable quality, cost, and time commitments. It requires improving the processes and establishing mechanisms to integrate the software early and often.

- **Keep getting better:** There is no such thing as the perfect or best or ideal process. Just when we think we have created the best process to address a problem, the external world changes and we must learn to quickly adapt to it. As the saying goes, "Today's solutions are tomorrow's problems." We must constantly keep looking for improvements rather than resting on yesterday's laurels.

Poppendieck's writings provide a number of insights to improve software development processes. While there might be a significant overlap in terms of ideas and the basic philosophy, lean doesn't really require any changes in the team's composition or its software process, per se, and these principles can be applied to an existing process—even in a waterfall process—in a Kaizen manner.

Kanban

Lean uses a rudimentary but rather effective tool, known as kanban, to create a pull system. The pull system ensures each part is only produced in the right quantity and only when it is actually needed. The same idea can be used in software development, too. Instead of developing and deploying all the features that might or might not have been asked for by the customer, we decide to deploy only those features that have a real customer ask. Everything else stays in the backlog, and we use work-in-progress limits at each step of the process to balance the pull system and achieve a continuous flow. In short, we throttle the number of cars that can get on the highway by ensuring that only a certain maximum number of cars are on the highway at any given time so that everyone can go faster.

In 2004–05, while working at Network General, Bangalore, I had to solve some significant problems around customer/field defects. When every method had failed us, we ended up writing a process that resembles a modern-day kanban. In all honesty, we stumbled upon it. I had then recently attended Tom Gilb's workshop on Evo,[17] and was eager to try Evo-style weekly deliveries. At that time, we were doing waterfall-style quarterly service packs. It took some serious thinking to craft a process that allowed us to pull the work off a common backlog and maintain a configuration management system that allowed developers and testers to ship on weekly cadence. It was a kanban in the sense that only when a developer would complete his bug fix, would he be allowed to pick up another. We didn't know the concept of "work in progress," but simply agreed to have a WIP=1 (which might or not be the best thing!).

---

[17]"Evolutionary Project Management," http://gilb.com/Project-Management

Luckily, it all worked out for us very well. We were extremely successful with our experiments. I have presented my work at various conferences since then, and the following slideshares refer to it in details:

- "Applying 'Kanban' in Enterprise-Class Products Sustaining Engineering: An Experience Report," Agile-Scrum International Summit 2012, Bangalore: www.slideshare.net/Managewell/applying-kanban-in-enterpriseclass-products-sustaining-engineering-an-experience-report

- "From Waterfall to Weekly Releases: A Case Study in Using Evo and Kanban (2004–05)," Agile India 2015, Bangalore: www.slideshare.net/Managewell/from-waterfall-to-weekly-releases

Around the same time, David J. Anderson created a Kanban process for knowledge work and service work, based on his team's work at Microsoft Hyderabad, India. His pioneering work led to the creation of a comprehensive body of knowledge, complete with frameworks, training, and certifications. This, in turn, led to the founding of the Lean-Kanban University (LKU). LKU has identified the following foundational principles and core practices of the Lean-Kanban Method.[18]

Foundational Principles

The Kanban Method identifies the following foundational principles that help establish the context in which a system under implementation could benefit:

- **Start with what you do now:** Kanban doesn't require a drastic change in your existing process. The idea is to be able to start from whatever is the existing process. To that end, the Kanban Method is less "disruptive" than agile methods.

- **Agree to pursue evolutionary change:** Rather than bring about big-bang changes, keep learning and make slow and steady changes to the process.

---

[18]"The Kanban Method," http://edu.leankanban.com/kanban-method

- **Initially, respect current roles, responsibilities, and job titles:** The Kanban Method doesn't require changing the team roles, structure, or titles, at least to begin with. Later on, as the process keeps improving, you might identify the need to change them, but there is no need to make radical changes as a pre-condition to the method.

- **Encourage acts of leadership at all levels:** The Kanban Method is generally aligned with the tenets of agility in terms of creating empowered teams that exhibit collective responsibility. To that end, leadership must not be restricted to the designated authority, but must be actively encouraged across the team.

Core Practices

In addition to the foundational principles, the following core practices help explain The Kanban Method as they are implemented in software projects:

- **Visualize:** In most cases, the project metrics and other data about the project's progress remain deeply buried inside verbose documents and status reports that are hardly ever useful. When the same information and data are visualized, the same data is represented in a much more actionable and meaningful form.

- **Limit WIP:** This is perhaps the most important difference between a Scrum task board and a kanban board—the explicit definition of "work-in-progress" limits. Establishing WIP limits allows for balancing the work across various workstations so that the wastes in the process can be minimized. An explicit WIP limit ensures that upstream processes don't drown downstream processes, or downstream processes don't sit idle just because some process steps have a higher throughput on a local level.

- **Manage flow:** The idea is not to rush the product out of the process faster but to create an even flow that allows for a much better utilization of resources in a pull system than simply shoving the workflow downstream against a push system. A smooth flow can manage demand and supply much more effectively, rather than needing to invest in building higher capacity for a temporary or a short-term higher demand only to leave unused surplus capacity against a low demand.

- **Make policies explicit:** By making policies explicit, we remove the guesswork and subjectivity in the process, thereby leading to reduced variability and unpredictability. This improves the ability to plan the work much more effectively, and to execute the plan with higher predictability.

- **Implement feedback loops:** A process can only be made better by incorporating feedback, and the shorter the feedback loops, the easier, faster, and cheaper it becomes to incorporate feedback. When such feedback loops are created at the entire shipment level, i.e., the small unit of work that leads to a customer value being shipped (and not just at the intermediate level of work completion), it ensures that the feedback is not just on a piecemeal basis but captures the entire process of creating and delivering customer value. If there are any issues during this process, a short feedback loop can help ensure that appropriate remedial action is taken without creating more parts with similar defects or issues.

- **Improve collaboratively, evolve experimentally** (using models and the scientific method): Finally, the Kanban Method places importance on team collaboration and experimentation to bring about changes incrementally.

The most important contribution of kanban in software engineering is providing a non-timebox option to incremental software development. Based on my own work in 2004–05, I learned that such a system works extremely well for problems where the work arrival pattern is stochastic in nature, as is the case for customer requests or field issues. Anderson's Kanban Method also advocates not estimating the work, though we did estimate our work and found it helpful in planning, especially during the QA phase when test setup availability could become a bottleneck.

I would strongly recommend Anderson's blue book on Kanban for any serious practitioner looking for ideas on a non-timebox way of delivering increments of software.

Agile Engineering Practices

Unlike linear or sequential engineering practices in a traditional waterfall project, agile advocates concurrent engineering. The idea is to take a little bit of task, perform just enough analysis, just enough design, implement and test it, and "deliver" it. However, let the phrase "just enough" not mislead you into thinking that we simply ship a low-quality piece of code! On the contrary, we ship the highest-quality code that we can create in that quantum of time—we just deliberately reduce the amount of functionality to what is most important to the customers. In that sense, we let quality prevail over quantity.

Secondly, we don't randomly pick just any functionality to be delivered. Agile places a very high importance on delivering the highest-value software in short and frequent intervals. This can't be accomplished without a clear-cut understanding of the business value each feature creates. Agile methods recognize that the value is created by differentiation and not by aggregating all features in one big lump of software.

The reason agile adopts this strategy is to accelerate the end-to-end software creation and expedite customer feedback. Let's understand why these are important. When we traverse the entire horizontal path of software creation (that is, analysis, design, coding, integration, and testing) as well as deliver a vertical slice of functionality (for example, user interface, business logic, middleware, database, and backend) in the smallest conceivable piece of demonstrable functionality, we create opportunities to mitigate several critical technical, infrastructure, and business risks that typically go uncontested in a traditional software project in the waterfall model till the final stages of integration and testing, by which time it is too late to incorporate any upstream changes without accepting serious time and effort implications.

It is highly possible that such early efforts lead to lots of problems and even to rejection of the early deliverables. Sometimes this can dissuade conventional teams who are not used to such adverse feedback early in the development lifecycle, and believe that they should only ship a fully-constructed and well-tested piece of software so that the shipment is "right first time", thereby eliminating the need for feedback. On the contrary, agile practitioners welcome such feedback, especially when it comes to integration and testing issues because it allows a course-correction process to begin that goes on until late in the release cycle, eventually leading to a far superior product and a greater customer and stakeholder experience. In the traditional project, all practitioners have is a documents-and-status reports to figure out. However, in an agile project, they are assured of working software at periodic intervals, and they can understand the system being built much better than lengthy Microsoft Word documents.

However, creating working software is not a science project. It requires high technical skills. Practitioners must be able to work with multiple unknowns and assumptions, while systemically creating high-quality engineering components.

Let's understand the key engineering processes and artifacts that help us accomplish this. We have used the Scrum framework and its associated artifacts to explain some of the underlying concepts. However, we don't advocate any specific process. We recommend that practitioners understand the core idea behind the concept being discussed, rather than picking up any ready-made solutions. As any serious agile practitioner knows, these ideas are only "training wheels"—great to get started when you are a novice, but as you gain proficiency and fluency, you want to replace these training wheels, or even completely eliminate them, so that you can develop processes and practices that suit your needs far better than the standard version offers.

User Requirements

An old saying goes that walking on water and working on product requirement are very easy—if only they were both frozen! The sad truth is that user requirements are never complete,[19] so if your process places that as a precondition, which the waterfall method did, you might be disappointed.

In Scrum, we represent user requirements in the form of "user stories" in a live document known as "product backlog" that is never complete or frozen (and hence never baselined in the traditional sense), but is prioritized according to what might be more value to the customers. Rather than waiting for long periods of time for them to be first complete before starting with the design and development, we start with what we know today, and build them in a way that subsequent changes can be accommodated with little pain. In each sprint, we take up the highest value stories that the team can deliver at a sustainable pace. We call this subset of the product backlog the sprint backlog, and the only condition we impose is that no changes can be made to this sprint backlog once the sprint gets underway.

User Stories

User stories are essentially a "tweet-length" representation of a key product functionality expressed from the point of view of a user. It deliberately skips finer details in favor of providing a general, high-level direction, for the agilests believe the value is not in documentation but in conversation. Given the obvious inadequacies of documentation (for example, natural languages are not mathematically complete or proven to be correct or unambiguous),

---

[19]One could argue that if the user requirements are indeed complete, the product that would be built might only represent the time when those requirements were thought of; however, it is very likely that the world has moved on since then.

agile practitioners favor identifying just the high-level stories that act as place-holders for a future conversation between the product owner and the concerned developers. This in-person conversation is a collaborative dialogue that enhances the richness of requirements that might otherwise take weeks.

Ron Jeffries proposed the 3C approach to write better user stories:

- **Capture:** A user story is typically small enough to be captured on a 4"x6" index card. The limited space places a physical limit on the number of details that might not be required at this stage. I like to use the "tweet-length" analogy so that only the most crucial elements of a user-facing requirement are captured.

- **Conversation:** Given that a user story will only capture the essence of what a user might want to accomplish with a given system, and a conversation might be needed to elicit these further details, the user story acts as an invitation for such later-date conversations.

- **Confirmation:** This suggests identifying the conditions of completion that will lead to successful acceptance by the product owner, including the non-functional requirements (NFR). Identifying these conditions upfront builds a level of transparency that allows the product owner and the teams to work on the same page.

This 3C framework is a nice way to describe the overall concept behind user story, but how does one determine if a given user story is good or bad?

In 2003, Bill Wake came up with a readiness criteria, called "INVEST"[20] to allow the product owner and the team to be on the same page:

- **Independent:** It should be possible to clearly identify a user story that is independent of other stories.

- **Negotiable:** The user story should only give a general direction of "what" is required without getting into "how" it is going to be implemented.

- **Valuable:** Sometimes also written as "vertical," a user story must be of value to the customer, that is, it creates some level of functionality that an end-user can use.

- **Estimable:** The user story is a key input for release and sprint planning, and hence it must be possible to estimate it using estimation methods.

---

[20]http://xp123.com/articles/invest-in-good-stories-and-smart-tasks/

- **Small:** Long user stories represent significant technical and project management risks. Thus, a good story should ideally complete inside a single iteration so that all the risks associated with it can be validated.

- **Testable:** A user story must be testable. In other words, its behavior and acceptance criteria must be clearly specified so that it can be demonstrated if the implementation meets all those requirements.

The teams could typically use INVEST readiness criteria during backlog grooming and sprint planning sessions to determine if the given user story needs any further refinement from the product owner, or if it is good to go. Some teams also plan an upfront release planning workshop where they can additionally use the INVEST criteria. The key is to recognize that whenever there are new or changed requirements, it represents a risk for planning the activities inside a release or a sprint. An instrument like INVEST should be used to understand and mitigate corresponding risks.

But, what do these user stories look like?

Agile practitioners have left this question open-ended to allow the teams to decide what format they would like to use. However, for those looking for some quick start guidance, the following is a very commonly used "template" for writing user stories:

As **<who>** I want to do **<what>**, so that **<why>**

where the three components are:

- **Who:** Who is the intended user of this feature? This is ideally represented as a user persona so that the elements of human-centered design are adequately represented in capturing the user requirements. By identifying the "who", we provide a context to the "what" which would otherwise reflect functionality but without really any human-centricity.

- **What:** What do they need to do with the feature? The functionality is not expressed as a system feature but how a given user persona interacts with the system to accomplish some task. Traditionally, we have expressed requirements only in terms of "what", which often left developers wondering why should anyone want that given functionality, etc.

- **Why:** Why do they need this feature? Determining the "why" helps establish the key reason a given user persona wants to use the given system. Establishing a proper "why" is extremely important to help developers understand the real reason a given "who" will require a given "what", or the business value they will accrue out of it.

User stories represent an unconventional way to communicate about user requirements. Without getting into very heavy details, the idea is to keep the central idea very lightweight, but encourage communication from all relevant team members as and when the right moment comes. To that end, user stories discourage excessive analysis upfront when the story hasn't quite been confirmed on the backlog. Thus, it is a very lean approach.

There is extensive literature,[21] and guidance[22] in the agile and Scrum community on how to write user stories. In this book, we have explained the context in which user stories are useful for agile product development. Compared to other methods of communicating that require traditional product requirements documents ("PRDs") or detailed "use cases", the user stories are short and crisp, and they invite collaboration. They also encourage innovation from the developers.

Splitting User Stories

What happens when a given user story is "big"? If the team proceeds with sizing it (say, using planning poker[23] or any other equivalent method), it might be unknowingly signing up for risk given that not all details inside the story might be visible or known in such a big story. So, it is in the entire team's, as well as the customer's interest, to break down stories to a more manageable size before making planning commitments. But, how do you split a user story?

The conventional wisdom of splitting user requirements along the horizontal layers of architecture is prone to challenges, as was identified back in 1968 by Mel Conway.[24] A horizontal way to specify requirements invariably leads to a layered architecture, which leads to longer lead times and other challenges. While this was the classical way to specify the architecture, agile methods favor vertical splitting alongside logical function of a cluster of feature boundaries, where each vertical split is a full-stack, end-to-end, customer-facing feature. This ensures that each piece of work that the team undertakes can indeed

---

[21]"User Stories: An Agile Introduction," www.agilemodeling.com/artifacts/userStory.htm
[22]"User Stories," www.mountaingoatsoftware.com/agile/user-stories
[23]"Planning Poker in Details," www.old-planningpoker.com/detail.html
[24]"How Do Committees Invent?," Melvin Conway, 1968, www.melconway.com/Home/Conways_Law.html

be delivered to the end-users, rather than completing an internal module or a component that might appear to give the sense of progress without really delivering working software.

One such method is the hamburger method[25] by Gojko Adzic. It uses the metaphor of how we eat a hamburger—we don't eat the top bread first and then the patty and then the tomato slice and the lettuce, and so on. Rather, we take a big vertical bite and in every bite, we get a bit of each of the layers of the hamburger! Similarly, when we apply the hamburger method, the idea is to identify components of each layer and recombine them in a way that allows for a full vertical slide of functionality to be delivered in each increment of delivery. It allows us to establish validation points—not just technical ones in terms of the tech-stack compatibility but also in terms of the customer feedback on functionality, usability, and performance. I like the method for its simplicity and flexibility. However, teams might discover more effective methods that are more contextual to their work. You can find some good guidance at this blog post on epic sharding.[26]

Estimating User Stories

Once we have split the user stories into an acceptable level (which doesn't have be a standard one-size-fit-all, but rather more suited to every team's comfort level), we are ready to estimate their size. In a traditional project management approach, we mostly adopt top-down methods that have their own limitations:

- **Expert judgment:** There might not be any substitute for an expert in the knowledge-intensive industry such as ours. However, an expert might not be always available and definitely won't lead to improving an organizational collective capability to do better estimations in future.

- **Parametric estimation:** If we could somehow come up with the size (say, as in lines of code or function points), we might be able to use something like the software equation[27] to compute the effort and duration. However, given the variability in human capabilities, is a one-size approach even useful?

---

[25]"Splitting User Stories: The Hamburger Method," http://gojko.net/2012/01/23/splitting-user-stories-the-hamburger-method/
[26]Epic Sharding, http://blog.pivotal.io/pivotal-labs/labs/epic-sharding

- **Analogous estimation:** If there are historical data points from similar projects in the past, it might be one way to do a kind of "estimation by reference." However, in all honesty, no two software projects are alike and such estimates might come with their own error margins.

We could also use bottom-up estimation methods but they also suffer from limitations:

- **Function point:** We might need to capture all requirements upfront and must know enough about all the requirements to compute the functions points with reasonable accuracy, not to mention that we must first train all developers to be experts on function points.

- **Wideband delphi:** It seems like a good way to crowdsource the knowledge and arrive at a collective opinion fairly quickly, except that too much time could be wasted in arriving at "precision" when just the "accuracy" will do.

- **Lines-of-code productivity/backfiring:** If we can compute the size in lines of code and we know the productivity data, we might be able to back-compute the effort and roll it up across rest of the phases. The process suffers from over-standardizing human capabilities and effort distributions across phases, which might not always be true.

- **Three-point estimates:** —Instead of a single data point, we could do three-point estimates[28] and triangulate the data to improve our estimates, which might be a bit better way to crowdsource the estimates.

However, from the historical data and literature, it doesn't seem like these approaches were very successful in giving us reliable estimates. As a result, it was common practice to add liberal amount of buffers in the estimates to improve the confidence levels, a practice that Eliyahu Goldratt discussed well in *The Critical Chain*.[29] Clearly, there are several limitations and biases affecting the estimates, and even then given the track record of project execution in our industry, no one is happy with what we have.

---

[27]"Software Equation," https://en.wikipedia.org/wiki/Software_equation
[28]https://en.wikipedia.org/wiki/Three-point_estimation
[29]"Critical Chain," www.goldratt.co.uk/resources/critical_chain/

Agile methods discard top-down methods as being too risky. This is in line with the overall lean thinking to reduce the batch size. As we discussed in previous sections, we break user stories until we feel they are small enough as per the INVEST criteria. What is small? Again, there is no single mathematical definition, but generally, small is something that could be reasonably accomplished inside a single sprint (and, there again, we are not talking about just barely fitting it inside a sprint!). We are looking at a something that is small enough to be taken through an entire cycle of closed-loop learning in a small time slice that ideally fits well inside a sprint length. We do it so that we can not only deliver something of value but also create data points that help execution of other stories better in terms of similar risks of technology, infrastructure, and customer asks.

Now that we have a small story, we need to estimate its size and effort. A size estimate allows us to get a sense of how much work needs to be done, and the effort gives us a sense of how much effort and time it would take to accomplish it. Quite often, we skip the size and directly proceed to effort. However, this is fraught with risks and several challenges. First off, the grain size of our work at the start of the project is too big to be broken down at such "inch-pebbles"[30] level, which is quite impractical and of not much utility. On the other hand, the size of a software is a very soft and abstract notion with high levels of uncertainty and error margins. On top of it all, the cone of uncertainty[31] trumps it all, even though the business expects hard commitments to be made about the project delivery. So, how do we proceed?

As Goldratt explained in *The Critical Chain*, we tend to pad our effort to increase the confidence level, and unfortunately, due to student syndrome,[32] the buffer gets exhausted first. Even if the work somehow gets done before the deadline, the time savings are not given back to the project (even though the delays do end up accumulating!). Now imagine an environment where sticking to estimates is considered non-negotiable. We will only end up seeing more people gaming the system by building in all kinds of invisible buffers, and we will never get a true sense of the "size" of the system to be developed for us to do any meaningful release planning.

Agile approach is to delink the size and effort. Size is the high-grain-size work items (such as features, epics, and stories) that can't be precisely estimated, but accurate-enough information about them (say, in a given ballpark) might be helpful to find similar, or comparable, work in the backlog and do an estimation for the entire release to get a high-order plan underway. The effort is

---

[30]"How to Use Inch-Pebbles When You Think You Can't," www.jrothman.com/articles/1999/01/how-to-use-inch-pebbles-when-you-think-you-cant/
[31]"The Cone of Uncertainty," www.construx.com/Thought_Leadership/Books/The_Cone_of_Uncertainty/
[32]"Student Syndrome," https://en.wikipedia.org/wiki/Student_syndrome

computed for small-grain-size work items (like individual tasks inside stories) that can be well estimated but only for the stories that are crystal clear in the near horizon of planning, that is, the sprint backlog items. So, they could be helpful only in planning and tracking the most immediate work. However, using those methods to estimate the entire product release backlog might be like using a tape measure to measure a football ground—it is neither going to be accurate nor useful to anyone. So, we use two different approaches to estimate the size of work—the first one is a relative sizing of the high-level work, while the second one is the absolute effort required for specific low-level tasks.

We need the right balance of accuracy and precision in our estimates. Unfortunately, we tend to mix them up without realizing they are not the same! The following diagram illustrates how they are different from each other. Imagine someone practicing target shooting. Depending on their skill level, we could broadly expect one of the four patterns shown in Figure 6-1.

While low accuracy, low precision estimates are useless to just about everyone, we do need the following during different stages of agile planning:

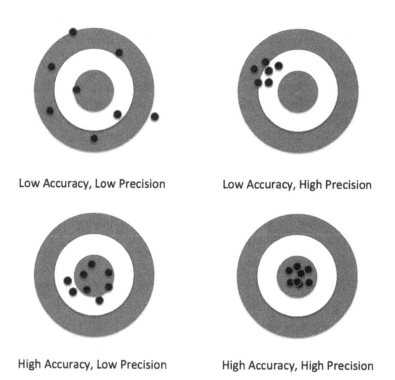

Low Accuracy, Low Precision   Low Accuracy, High Precision

High Accuracy, Low Precision   High Accuracy, High Precision

Figure 6-1. Varying skill levels could lead to variances in accuracy and precision

- **High accuracy, low precision:** –When we are looking at the product release backlog and want to know when can we get this entire backlog completed, we don't need to be precise to the second decimal place. It is good enough to know the ballpark estimates with enough accuracy. As long as we don't change the measurement scale halfway through a release, we can establish a measurement system to help us plan the release using big rocks at that level.

- **Low accuracy, low precision; low accuracy, high precision, and high accuracy, high precision:** When we start to work on a new project and everyone on the team is new to the work, we can expect low accuracy, low precision estimates. Over time, we share our learning with each other and establish common standards of workmanship and graduate to low accuracy, high precision because everyone is now aligned to what the task entails. As the team continues to get better with understanding and predicting its work and acquires higher standards of the workmanship (that is, a more stringent "definition of done"), it matures to high accuracy, high precision stage.

However, I must call out that the capability is not the only factor that impacts this journey. The environment, empowerment, and fear of reprisal in case of mistakes could all have a significant impact on how people actually behave, individually or in a group. Estimation is not a mechanical activity. If anything, it is a social activity. We need a mechanism that allows us to initially arrive at high accuracy, low precision estimates of size and later, as we go to the finer details, allows us to plan the most immediate work using high accuracy, high precision estimates.

One of the most popular techniques to estimate the size of work is using the so-called planning poker cards. Essentially a variant of the wideband delphi technique, which uses Fibonacci series as the grading scale, the technique relies on crowdsourcing estimates such that the following biases are minimized, if not completely eliminated:

- Bias of group think

- Bias of expert opinion. In a team, there might be individuals with specific expertise.

- Bias of effort vs. schedule

The output of a planning poker session is typically expressed in terms of a unitless size known as story points, rather than in hours. Story points are abstract numbers that prevent premature commitment and gaming, but are fairly useless by themselves unless they are viewed in the context of other story point estimates by the same team for the same release. They represent the relative size of a story as per the acceptance criteria and team's definition of done compared to some previously agreed-upon story in the same release. Story points are helpful for long-range and mid-range planning—not for the work to be done "here and now." For that, we must consider breaking down stories into individual tasks, as described in the next section.

Breaking Down Stories into Tasks

As we saw in the previous section, story points are useful in the high-level planning of a release, but when it comes to implementing a story, it must be broken down into its constituent technical tasks,[33] for example, writing a new class, or refactoring the database. These technical tasks are well known to the development team, and they are in great position to estimate them directly in hours. Breaking-down of the stories into tasks allows for the technical details about implementation emerge, which helps in better task estimation and planning, as well as risk reduction. However, it is key to recognize that tasks can't really be verified. They must be carried out and tested by the respective developer for the correctness of desired operation, but they must be collated alongside other tasks that are part of the same story. Only then can we apply the acceptance criteria to test it at a story level for functionality and usability. However, establishing tasks creates a basis for making and measuring tangible progress on a daily basis. Identifying and implementing the individual technical tasks is the least count of a developer's progress that has no real meaning to anyone outside the team.

There is no single magic formula for how to break down stories into tasks; however, there is good guidance available for it, like this one.[34] Most techies can decompose a story into its constituent technical tasks, though given the massive number of combinations and permutations in a modern-day tech stack, it is likely that one might always forget to include all the components during planning. I find that involving the entire team in the breaking down of stories into tasks is a great way to not only remove the guesswork from the process, but also share the tacit knowledge without the need to do excessive documentation. The second valuable learning is about keeping the tasks small. A good guide is to stick to tasks that can be completed in less than one day (that is, a net productive programmer day, whatever that might be for your

---

[33]"The Difference between a Story and a Task," www.mountaingoatsoftware.com/blog/the-difference-between-a-story-and-a-task
[34]"How to Decompose User Stories into Tasks," www.payton-consulting.com/decompose-user-stories-tasks/

team). This ensures a feedback loop at the end of the day to confirm whether the task was completed as envisaged, and thus minimize the technical tasks and associated risks to go into the next day.

For each of these tasks, the team estimates the effort directly in hours. These estimates are then compared to the total number of productive or net hours available to the team throughout the upcoming sprint and accordingly committed. This process helps balance the effort available vs. the effort required to complete tasks and deliver stories at the end of the sprint.

Backlog Grooming

In Scrum, a product backlog is a prioritized wish list of all features. It is always considered "emergent," meaning we never consider a situation where all requirements might be known to the customer or the team, and we could "baseline" them once and for all (and utilize the money-making "change management" process for any subsequent changes). Rather, we recognize the inevitability—and the power—of constantly changing requirements as the means to eventually deliver the "right" software by a series of feedback cycles.

On a well-run team, just about anyone might be empowered to add ideas to the product backlog—even the development team members. And they might submit ideas throughout the time a product is alive. Now we don't expect all ideas worthy of being taken up, so Scrum recommends that we trust the product owner to make that call. The product owner might or might not individually be the most competent expert to make that call by herself. However, she is expected to work with other folks from business and engineering to collect all data points so that we could make the "most-informed" call.

Scrum requires a sprint be planned on the first day of each sprint. However, over time, practitioners have found that by simply focusing on the current sprint and ignoring the needs of the most immediate future—the next upcoming sprint—we limit our ability to not just prepare and plan for it, but also make the entire planning a rather episodic one, even if only in shorter timeboxes! So, the practitioners advocate a more continuous discussion of the emerging backlog as and when new features are requested. Teams typically spend an hour or so each week discussing major new changes in the product backlog since the previous week. If the changes are clear and small enough, even estimate its size, so that the product owner can use this information in the overall release plans. I have seen teams taking an hour each week, as well as teams taking ten minutes every day, to conduct backlog grooming.

Irrespective of what works best for you, the key takeaway from such backlog grooming is to keep the team engaged on the upcoming changes and to help the product owner do a continuous release planning based on emergent changes. This ensures there are no, or minimum, surprises to anyone in the end.

In a steady state, the backlog grooming sessions help a team maintain a lookahead of one to two sprints while also exploring the product backlog and helping the product owner "groom" the backlog—break down epics, estimate the stories that appear to be ready (that is, as per the INVEST criteria), reconsider any need to reprioritize stories, and so on.

User Story Mapping (USM)

A prioritized product backlog is a great way to represent stories in a one-dimensional list on the basis of their relative values and, thus, establish a basis for scheduling them in sprints. However, a backlog might not be the most effective in terms of capturing a sense of the system being designed. For example, an isolated story that is priority #2 might not have anything to do with its adjoining stories on #1 and #3 positions in terms of its logical placement across the product's functionality. So, a developer working on the #2 story might not get the entire picture of the functionality that the story #2 is a part of, nor will she ever get to realize that the given subset of functionality is actually composed of stories #2, #8, #14, and #23. Similarly, the stories #1, #4, #9, #19, and #51 might collectively represent another functionality. Even if we simply go on scheduling the stories per the priority in the product backlog, we might be completing stories and yet not shipping value from the user's point of view!

Jeff Patton came up with an interesting way to bunch user stories in a two-dimensional map rather than placing them in order of priority. He calls it User Story Mapping.[35] He felt there was an opportunity to cluster them based on a higher-order grouping, or a theme. He propounded that such grouping created a better opportunity to understand the big picture and then build increments than to deliver higher-value stories that might not help build a minimum functionality.

A user-story map, or USM, is essentially a view of all user stories in a release (or a series of releases) that has been simultaneously prioritized on time and priority, as shown in Figure 6-2.

---

[35]"User Story Mapping," www.agileproductdesign.com/presentations/user_story_mapping/

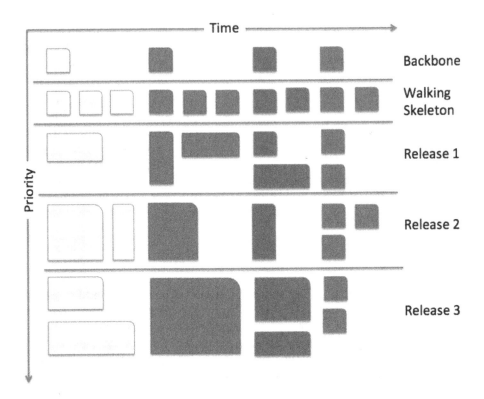

Figure 6-2. A user-story map organizes user stories based on a timeline and priority

We initially identify the "backbone," which gives a structure to the solutions being discussed. These could be the big-bucket functionalities that a system requires. To accomplish the backbone, we might have a number of features that are broken down into epics and stories. The bare minimum set of stories that represents a viable solution is identified and is known as the "walking skeleton." It could be conceptually equivalent to identifying the Minimum Viable Product (MVP). All other stories are prioritized into the "release slices," which help stagger the releases without losing the information within a respective backbone grouping.

Jeff Patton wrote a book on this, and has given further guidance on his web site.[36]

---

[36]"User Story Mapping," http://jpattonassociates.com/user-story-mapping/

Design, Development, and Testing

In the waterfall model (Figure 6-3), we take up a phased approach to software development. Following the requirements analysis phase where we typically document requirements into use cases or verbose descriptions of the system behavior, there is a documentation-intensive phase where the design of the system is specified. It is described typically in the form of UML diagrams, event-trace diagrams, a high-level architecture, or in Word documents. These documents are then taken as the input by developers for development, coding, or the implementation phase. (See Figure 6-3.)

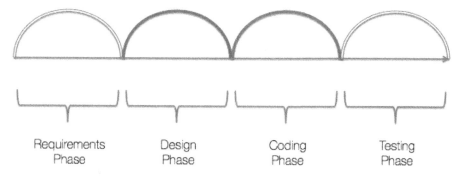

Requirements Phase   Design Phase   Coding Phase   Testing Phase

Figure 6-3. In the waterfall model, the engineering phases are sequential to each other

In the past, there would typically be high-level-design (HLD) phase followed by a low-level-design (LLD) phase. The HLD phase would establish the architecture and identify big building blocks or sub-systems. The LLD would go on to describe key class hierarchy, public methods, and even the algorithms, pseudocode, data structures, and so on. Finally, when the developers were done with the coding phase, they would start unit testing, which used be manual more often than not. Once the developer was satisfied with the results of unit testing at the white-box level, she would get its code reviewed and then check in. Not every check-in would always be built, but when the build would be done, there would be all kinds of integration issues, often leading to finger pointing and a waste of countless hours. Finally, when the build was completed, the QA team member would execute functional testing at the black-box level, which once again would be highly manual and, hence, could only be done on the "QA drops." QA drops were mini-episodic events where the entire system under development was built and given to QA for a round of functional or regression testing. Not only was this entire process extremely time-intensive, it was also very inflexible. Any agility that might be expected at the developer level was out of question.

Instead of performing such "sequential" engineering, agile methods advocate concurrent engineering (Figure 6-4)—that is, perform design, development, and testing concurrently to minimize the intermediate steps and eliminate phase-driven hand-offs. Instead of taking on 100% requirements and then completing 100% analysis, followed by 100% design, then 100% coding and finally 100% testing, agile methods favor taking a very small subset of those requirements but completing all engineering activities for that subset in the smallest amount of time. Ideally, a very small number of individuals works together to complete these activities. The result is not a heavy document but a piece of well-tested code that takes far less time to develop but delivers a high-quality, customer-facing functionality.

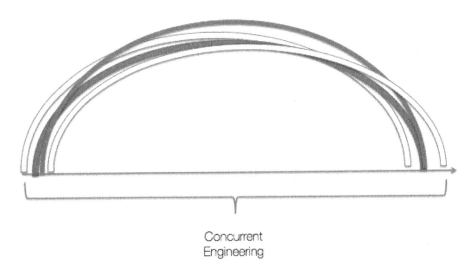

Concurrent
Engineering

Figure 6-4. In agile development, the emphasis is on undertaking all aspects of engineering in a concurrent manner

The typical sequence of design, development, and testing is reversed in this approach. As described in Figure 6-5, a developer takes a small task (that has already been broken down inside the user story) and, before starting anything else, writes the test case to test its desired performance. Such a test-first approach is based on the idea that the human mind is likely to become biased during testing to subconsciously conform to the way an implementation has been done. This is known as test-driven development, or TDD. So, if we first specify the test cases, we are less likely to fall into the familiarity trap. In terms of implementation, a TDD approach ensures that at any point in time, a suite of automated unit test cases is available to test a given piece of functionality. This gives a great deal of power to a developer to go out and make any changes to the code because she is never more than a few changes away from validating whether any changes made break the existing functionality.

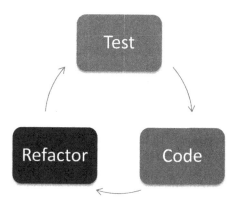

Figure 6-5. The test-code-refactor loop helps build high-quality software in a series of small iterations

This piece of test code is not very elaborate—maybe a few lines, but enough to test the module's key functional behavior to be created. Predictably, this piece of test code will fail because there is no functionality in terms of the production code to test it against. Immediately after writing the test code, the developer writes the functional code that will satisfy the test code enough to pass the test cases. Again, the emphasis is on writing the absolute least amount of code that will make the test cases pass. Once that is done, the developer now refactors the code, that is, redesigns the code to improve its design, readability, performance, and so on. However, unlike a traditional redesign, this effort might at most be limited to a dozen or two lines of code at a time and immediately proceeds with executing the test loop. Such a "test-code-refactor" or "red-green-refactor" loop might be typically executed every hour or even more frequently, and it leads to a software whose state is always known relative to the previous stable state. The software is continually "grown" around like an expanding spiral. When the entire module is ready, the developer checks in the code in a code repository, or a configuration management system, which is then hooked on to a continuous integration (CI) server. Each such check-in typically leads to a CI build that gives quick feedback if any major functionality of the code is broken. Along with each such a CI build, an automated build verification test suite might also be executed that tests the completed work at story level. The CI build as well as the build verification test are both executed in fast cycles, typically not more than 8–10 minutes or faster, so that the developers don't have to wait for hours or days to get feedback on their software.

This test-code-refactor loop represents the smallest unit of concurrent engineering at a task level. When the task is completed, it is integrated with other modules to test the integration (rather than doing a traditional big-bang integration). When all modules pertaining to a story have been completed, we can demonstrate and test a user story—the small subset of user-facing functionality. Unlike waterfall model where testing is a phase downstream in the development process, agile emphasizes building in quality upfront. At its core, it does that by reducing the length of the feedback loop as much as possible so that establishing the cause-and-effect relationship between a bug and the defect is easier to establish.

In terms of product validation, agile also places heavy emphasis on building small but complete increments of functionality and delivering them to the customer for earlier feedback. In case the feedback doesn't match expectations, there is an opportunity to correct the course sooner and at a cheaper cost. In the worst-case scenario, the product increment doesn't meet any requirements and the team can make necessary changes much earlier in the cycle, thereby minimizing the amount of time and money wasted.

This could be accomplished using techniques such as Acceptance Test—Driven Testing (ATDD), where the system under development might be subjected to automated tests at a system level. These test cases are oblivious to the internal implementation of its features and are only interested in ascertaining whether the system under development meets those pre-specified criteria. This could ensure that the feedback loop is shortened so that developers could get feedback at each epic or a feature-level sooner than later.

Behavior-Driven Development (BDD) is yet another idea that seeks to specify and test a system's behavior in plain English. However as an idea, agile seeks to establish continuous feedback at appropriate levels of a system, and it is possible to eliminate a testing or a validation phase the way it exists today. Using the ideas of test-driven development at all levels of software, and using the power of automated tests and frameworks, the system under development can be subjected to continuous automated testing that can reduce the unit size of product validation to each story, thus paving the way for incremental or continuous delivery if the users are willing to accept incremental functionality.

Conclusion

In the waterfall-development paradigm, we often estimated and made plans when we knew the least about the system. Hidden buffers invariably compensated for this, giving a false sense of precision, even if the estimates themselves were not accurate. The engineering methods were documentation-led because they worked on the older economics of software development that one hour of computing time is costlier than one hour of programmer time. Consequently, we must use the programmer time to optimize the computing time by doing extensive documentation and review it to ascertain program correctness. Given the siloed nature of software development in such a model, we often had to accept extremely long loops of feedback, and the risk of it all blowing up would be extremely high towards the integration and testing phases.

However, over time, the computing time has become substantially cheaper compared to the programmer time, so it doesn't make sense to do extensive documentation simply to communicate the requirements or review the design—it is far cheaper and effective to simply write software and test it. However, it must be done in quick enough bursts that allow for rapid feedback and course correction, i.e. correct before making the same mistake again! Unfortunately, traditional engineering methods don't lend themselves very well to such in-process course correction because the developers and testers must rely on costly and laborious manual processes to verify and validate after every change. Agile favors a concurrent engineering approach where the test-first mindset creates a basis for comparing the "before" and "after" condition with minimal effort. More importantly, the automated test cases that are created as part of the development also grow incrementally and become a permanent part of the code, which unlike the documentation, are always in sync with the code and, thus, more likely to be used. The result is a well-tested and working piece of software created at every sprint, and if the system-level validation is also possible at each sprint, then even delivering those "potentially shippable increments".

In Chapter 7, we will discuss how we apply principles of agile product development to deliver the software to customers.

Deliver

Not documents ... but the software!

Give your clients the earliest delivery consistent with quality—whatever the inconvenience to us.

—Arthur C. Nielsen

In the past, a long waterfall-style development was briefly punctuated by the delivery of documents such as the design documents and status reports. It finally culminated with the real end goal—the software delivery. The documents were often seen as the proxy for the real product because nothing else was available to communicate progress through the long dark phases proceeding the final delivery. Needless to say, these documents often had no correlation whatsoever to the actual product or its quality. A status report could at best only communicate the past (which everyone already knew!), but never really predict the future in ways that would be meaningful to the product development team and the customers so that they could collectively re-plan their activities to align with the evolving dynamics of a project.

In this final chapter, we will examine how agile product development enters the final phase in which being able to make a high-quality delivery becomes most critical. During this phase, the customers don't care what agile methodology you used during development or what tools your team used. As far as they are concerned, the software should just work—not just when doing the initial installation, but every time it is accessed.

After all, the proof is in the pudding!

Integration

One particularly sore point of waterfall-style development was integration. All along the development phases, the software was written by individual developers in silos on their respective desktops. Only when the integration phase began would the team start to "integrate" the software modules together—and then all hell would break loose. What should ideally be a non-event in terms of assembling different parts of software would soon turn into days and weeks of saga with all its frustration and unpredictability. In several cases, the integration would rapidly degenerate into a mini-project by itself! As you can imagine, in such a development process, the customer became a distant second-class citizen, whose interests were hardly the driving point of software delivery. However, none of this has to be this way, at least not anymore.

Compared to these rather obviously questionable and, thankfully, obsolete delivery methods, agile methods seek to deliver incremental value throughout the lifecycle—literally from the first iteration onward. As we discussed in Chapter 6, each iteration typically leads to high-quality working software of a subset of the final functionality—something that the customer can play around with and hopefully deploy in the production environment, which will lead to quality feedback. However, in the real world, the working software might be necessary but not sufficient to constitute a "delivery," especially when we consider every single iteration. For example, a team might complete a few stories over an iteration that meet their respective acceptance criteria, but have a limited utility for the users given the partial functionality it delivers. So, clubbing of individual stories into a full-fledged feature makes sense until we create complete functionality instead of shipping elements of code that only represent partial functionality. But even then, it is a big step forward from the older process.

Shipping

In the pre-Internet days, companies would typically ship software in CDs (floppies or tapes in the pre-CD days). Given the challenges and expenses of the physical shipment of CDs to customers all over the world, it is not surprising that such an episodic event was avoided. Since a CD could not be shipped every few weeks even if individual features were ready (which obviously they were not, as the waterfall-style didn't lend itself to completion and delivery of partial functionality), it was more like accumulating all the features for a mega-release every couple of years, and then delivering minor updates and repairs every couple of quarters. Due to the logistics and costs of shipping CDs, every amount of caution would need to be taken to ensure that bad code was not being delivered, lest another expensive operation be needed to ship a rectified code—at no additional costs to the customers. At some point, this last mile of delivery became the rate-limiting factor of the software development process and had a major impact on everything upstream. In other words, the tail started to wag the dog, and the upstream development process had to adapt itself to deliver a software that adhered 100% to the specs and delivered the right quality. However, as we have discussed before, this was wishful thinking given the nature of software development. There is ample data from the industry to suggest that the approach of first specifying every single requirement and then inspecting and testing every line of code after it was written wasn't the best way to ensure that the goals of software development were met.

When the Agile Manifesto came along in 2001, it emphasized the importance of "early and continuous delivery of valuable software." It discouraged a single episodic release that would typically be fraught with multiple "single points of failure". At that time, software configuration management practices were already beginning to mature. It was normal for teams to practice things such as daily builds (or rather, nightly builds) earlier in the lifecycle, followed by smoke tests to validate the integrity of these builds. However, these checks and balances were meant to get a continuous in-process feedback into what was still a waterfall-style delivery. Most of this software was never shipped until the time everything was ready to be shipped.

And then the Internet happened.

Among other things, the advent of the Internet created the possibility of delivering software globally without having to ship physical CDs. The end users simply had to access a web site in order to use the software. Whenever a patch, an update, or a new feature was ready, all the developers needed was a way to update the software that powered the web site and then the users would get the latest software. The end users didn't have to wait for the so-called "forklift upgrades" anymore—piecemeal updates were actually possible without any of the traditional costs and logistic issues of the past. Of course, the success of this new delivery method depended on whether the customers were willing to accept it. Given the short lead-times and relative ease of incremental upgrades, and the substantially lower risks of each of these upgrades, it is a no-brainer that users prefer them.

Cloud computing and SaaS have taken the paradigm further down the road. The customers and end users don't need to install the software on their devices. Instead, they simply access the web site whenever they want to use the software. The latest version of software is always available. Of course, in the mobile world, we are seeing a strong play of native apps, but the mobile Internet still continues to be the predominant form of accessing the software, having exceeded desktop Internet usage sometime during 2014–15.

Today's software delivery is not just about completing the coding and then shipping it via CDs. Given the increasing amount of software being hosted in private or public clouds that operate out of globally located data centers with hundreds of thousands of servers, the complexity of delivering a software at

Internet-scale becomes a significant challenge. This challenge is found not just at the technical level, but also at the business level.

Intel has a very interesting graphic on its web page: "What happens in an Internet minute?"[1] When you realize the sheer volume of the data being created and shared every single minute, you soon understand that traditional software delivery methods aren't adequate in this world. We need a way to deliver software that address today's needs:

- **Speed:** the speed of doing business in today's world, where every passing hour creates some new technology or business paradigm, and where decisions must be made in nano-seconds

- **Scale:** more and more businesses today are operating globally and, eventually, any serious business must consider performance at Internet-scale

- **Sustainability:** with more software being delivered online, there is an inevitable need to deliver and sustain a high-performance through the troughs and valleys of market demand

The developers cannot compromise quality since the technology, markets, and customer needs continue to evolve around the clock. Today, the leading software companies operate at high levels of speed, scale, and sustainability. They use their high performance to continuously deliver "wow" customer experiences.

Let's examine the building blocks in software development that enable software construction leading to the eventual delivery.

Software Configuration Management (SCM)

For a telecom project I worked on in 1995, we didn't use any code management tool at all. All of us wrote C++ code on our respective desktops. When we finished, we simply copied our .cpp and other resource files on a common desktop into pre-designated folders. Initially, we copied our individual work approximately every week and, later on, daily as we got close to completing the coding. Not every developer was able to "check in" their code daily (sometimes due to a bad developer behavior and sometimes due to interdependent modules that had to be significantly mocked up just to make the build

---

[1]www.intel.in/content/www/in/en/communications/internet-minute-infographic.html.

happen painlessly). Most of the time, we were not able to perform a build on this software during the initial days of the coding phase. However, we kept a local backup on a separate machine—just in case! We eventually completed the development, tested it rigorously, and packaged the software. One of our colleagues then traveled to the client location with the CD in hand. While installing the software, she discovered that our software wouldn't even install. After some debugging, we discovered that someone had changed the name of one of the database fields. Somehow, this had not affected the work during the preceding phases. Unfortunately, we had never tested the software on a "virgin" machine until installation.

After some Hollywood-style heroics, we did manage to save the day, but not before realizing that our configuration management, integration, build process, and packaging verification process were basically broken. We were lucky to come out with minor bruises that we could debug and fix fast. For example, we didn't even have backup in those days—the code repository was stored in file folders on one desktop and we would simply back up the repository onto another desktop! I don't know too many teams who were doing things very differently back then.

Clearly, we have come a long way.

With the advancement in software configuration management and build tools, all this sounds like a relic of a bygone era. A software configuration management system, or SCM (also known as a version control system), is a given today. With the advent of so many open source and free tools available, the SCM is largely a non-issue.

Over time, we got better tools (both free ones like CVS as well as paid ones like Rational (now IBM) ClearCase or Microsoft Visual SourceSafe, etc.) that made life much easier. We elevated the process rigor to include additional checks and balances where the tools lacked in capability. For example, during the late 90s, it was not uncommon to perform elaborate CMM- and ISO9000-style Physical Configuration Audits (PCAs) and Functional Configuration Audits (FCAs) to validate how well a configuration management environment was maintained for a project. These issues are still important, but most of these elements are available out-of-box with modern-day configuration management tools. We must remember that these are, at best, a side issue that must be quickly streamlined and automated so that developers don't waste time doing things that don't add any value to the product. Instead, they can focus on what does matter—creating innovative products.

In classical agile (that is, the Agile Manifesto), there is no specific recommendation on practice or tools around SCM. I believe the agilests saw that as an integral part of software development that didn't have to be explicitly called out. As a result, we don't have any CMM- or ISO-style guidelines on what to expect. The focus is on establishing and nurturing an environment that enables sustainable agility as a mindset and a set of values and practices. To that end, each team must identify and assess its needs rather and evolve its methods, process and tools than blindly following some standard tool or process.

However, specific agile frameworks such as DSDM and FDD do call out SCM explicitly. DSDM Atern doesn't specify a specific process or a tool to accomplish SCM, but it does talk about the following values of good configuration management[2]:

- Focus on business needs
- Deliver on time
- Collaborate
- Never compromise quality
- Build incrementally from firm foundations
- Develop iteratively
- Communicate continuously and clearly
- Demonstrate control

Similarly, FDD also talks about configuration management as a best practice without specifying any further details about the process per se. However, by the time FDD came out in 1997, SCM was already a commonplace activity, even in the waterfall world (thanks to Software CMM and ISO9000 TickIT). So, agile or no agile, anyone doing any non-trivial software development was probably practicing some form of configuration management. I remember that in the late 90s, all my teams had one engineer spending part of his time setting up and managing the configuration management environment, and for larger project teams, there was a full-time engineer managing the configuration, build and release environment.

If a good SCM solution was the minimum expectation 15 years ago, today it has been upgraded to Continuous Integration (CI).

Continuous Integration (CI)

In traditional software development, the standard practice was to have a prolonged coding phase followed by a relatively quick "big-bang" integration phase (talk about perennial optimism in our industry!). This sounded good in theory, but it almost always bombed in reality. As you can imagine, the process was fraught with risks. When multiple engineers were writing code

---

[2] "Configuration Management," www.dsdm.org/content/24-configuration-management.

without integrating their work collectively at regular intervals, serious issues arose whenever they decided to build the entire software. Even with initial agreements on who would do what, what interfaces would be provided, and how their signatures would look, as well as the testing of the individual components, they would not integrate together. Unfortunately, these issues would be discovered so late in the game that what should have been a non-event often became a project unto itself. Integration of the code was as painful as pulling teeth.

"Integration hell"[3] was real and often led to the last-mile problems of software delivery. As a result, people started integrating the code a bit sooner— during the (latter part of) coding phases without waiting for the completion of the entire coding phase. In this model, the developers would continue writing code, often in their private branches, and only check in every few days (or even weeks!), if at all. The builds would typically be more like distant events but more frequent than the erstwhile big-bang integration. Surely this led to improvements over big-bang integration, though it was only a half-step. Like several other practitioners who would tinker around with process and tools at that time, I also had an interesting experience.

In 1997, we stumbled upon a very rudimentary form of "Continuous Integration" while solving a real issue. We were using good old CVS for configuration management of our Oracle-based product for hospitals, and my team had close to 20 developers. It was based on client-server architecture and, thus, it was relatively easy to write it independently for developers as long as the server-side changes were centrally coordinated. So, even though there was a high level of agility at the developers' level, we didn't integrate them all together very frequently. With so much code being written, it was only natural that there would be some server-side and client-side issues whenever we would build, which would invariably lead to last-minute action and missed deadlines. To address the issue, we created a low-tech solution. Each time someone would commit the code, a copy of the module being checked in would be made in another common folder where all the latest versions of the entire codebase were kept. The developer could then trigger a manual build to check if his software was integrating with rest of the team's. We thought it was a smart solution that made it easier to verify if the software integrated well. Little did we realize that what we did brought us closer to modern-day Continuous Integration.

---

[3] "Continuous Integration: How to Avoid 'Integration Hell,'" https://dzone.com/articles/continuous-integration-how-0.

So, what is Continuous Integration, or CI? Martin Fowler defined[4] it in the following way:

> *Continuous Integration is a software development practice where members of a team integrate their work frequently, usually each person integrated at least daily—leading to multiple integrations per day. Each integration is verified by an automated build (including test) to detect integration errors as quickly as possible.*

Paul Duvall provided a short and sweet definition of CI in his 2007 book *Continuous Integration*: "build software at every change." Most developers are used to compiling their piece of software at frequent intervals, but they don't always go on to build the entire software. They are hesitant because they fear long build cycles and dozens of unresolved interdependencies lurking in the darkness, which would make the entire effort so time-consuming and effort-intensive that it wouldn't be of meaningful value as a source of continuous feedback. However, a well-implemented CI system could change all that.

CI originally started as one of the 12 practices within XP. Although it doesn't require nor recommend any specific tooling, teams normally use one of the several dozen commercial and open sources tools available. They all have a similar function. They work in tandem with the software configuration management system and, whenever there is a code check-in, an automated build on the CI server is triggered. This CI build is typically meant to be very fast—terms such as "espresso builds" are not uncommon to highlight that the build must be completed in the amount of time it takes to drink a coffee. The logic here is that if something isn't fast enough to give meaningful feedback to the developers, most likely it will be avoided and skipped. So, the idea is to make it usable by making it lightning fast. Once the build is ready, an automated test suite, typically known as Build Verification Test, is triggered to perform smoke testing on the build as well as regression testing on the existing code with some level of functional testing increases as newer features and stories are added to the newly checked-in code. Again, the goal is to keep it fast. I often see that teams have improved the builds to under ten minutes, but the verification takes between six and eight hours. In such situations, the developers will have no motivation to exploit the capabilities of the CI system, and the practice might deteriorate to a daily build (because an eight-hour build verification can only be run when everyone is asleep!).

---

[4]"Continuous Integration," http://martinfowler.com/articles/continuousIntegration.html.

In theory, CI can be practiced in just about any project—waterfall or agile. However, when implemented in the context of agile product development, it is specifically useful in building and testing the features incrementally. When we define byte-size stories at the planning level, we create the possibility to maintain the same small batch size during the development and through the integration—and achieve single-piece flow in product development. Remember the readiness criteria for user stories, "INVEST," where "I" stands for *independent*. If the stories have been well defined and are independent enough, they will be easier to implement and test without requiring significant amounts of code being available from any dependent features or stories. Second, when the acceptance criteria of those stories are clearly spelled out as part of the sprint planning (or as early as backlog grooming), it makes writing automated tests at the functional level much easier. So, while the developers go about developing the functionality, the test engineers can write automated test scripts that go on to be part of the build verification test suite. Every time the CI build is triggered, the entire system gets tested—not just for the newly added functionality but also for any regression effects on the existing functionality.

Each such integration is really a mini-integration with an additional increment of software added since the previous integration, but with a significantly lower risk of anything going wrong because we have already traversed the entire path of performing the integration and build and, thus, already know the last stable state of the software code. And when things do go wrong and a build breaks, it is far easier to debug and fix the problem since the quantum of change is much smaller.

A CI system can deliver continuous feedback per story (rather than on traditional monolithic software modules) that significantly reduces the need for a very complex big-bang integration. As Jez Humble and David Farley say in their 2011 book *Continuous Delivery*, "if it hurts, do it more frequently, and bring the pain forward." However, the risks relating to user experience or some assumptions around the key functional behavior of a feature might still remain untested because the output of a CI build might not be exposed to the customers unless deployed in the field. That's where the next two topics of continuous delivery and continuous deployment help push the boundaries.

Continuous Delivery

Hardly a day goes by when an app on your favorite mobile or tablet doesn't get an "update." In fact, when I pick up my tablet after not using it for several days, I can see a dozen or more updates waiting. At that point, I make the choice of whether to spend (some people might even call that "waste") the first 15 minutes updating to the latest version of those products, or use the apps and ignore the updates. What's happening here?

Welcome to the world where software is literally being released as it is being written. As a software developer, I now have the opportunity to keep writing software. Whenever a meaningful amount of product updates are ready, I club them up and make them available as a product update. Rather than making my software updates available once in a blue moon as was the practice in the past, I can now make them available "continuously." The user can decide if she would like to update her software immediately or continue to use the old software. Of course, over time, the old software will have reduced the ability to exploit newer hardware and operating system features and might even become incompatible with newer features.

Humble describes continuous integration in the following way:

> *Continuous integration demands that we are able to keep the application working after every change made to it. This includes changes to the structure or content of our data. Continuous delivery demands that we must be able to deploy any successful release candidate of our application, including the changes to the database, into production."*

The aim of continuous delivery is to always have a system in releasable state. If we go back to agile thinking, it takes the whole idea of delivering "vertical" stories through the end. However, we may not always deploy those changes into production. But, what if we were to actually deploy them?

Continuous Deployment (CD)

Most of us use dozens of consumer Internet software every day, such as Facebook, LinkedIn, Twitter, Google, and Flickr, and so on. Do you know what version of these services you are using at any given time? More than likely, you don't know, and probably no one else knows (not that it matters from the user point of view anymore!). We have moved away from the classical "version-and-release" mindset to a world where there is a constant "drip feed" of byte-sized features. Whenever a user logs onto the web site of an online or a hosted service or software, she receives the latest version of the software that is in production (which might constantly keep changing as she uses it, by the way!). With software apps (or native apps in the case of mobile), these increments of functionality were made available as notifications to the users and the choice to update was typically left to them. But with online services and software, the software makers can directly take care of software upgrades and, as a result, make the process even faster.

Any idea how much time it takes for companies to roll out such code updates into production?

At the Velocity 2011 Conference, Jon Jenkins shared Amazon's May Deployment Stats.[5] He said that every 11.6 seconds, someone at Amazon was deploying the code into production. He also mentioned that on average, some 10,000 hosts would receive a deployment. However, in that particular month, that number maxed up to 30,000. While I am sure those numbers have gone up significantly since then, I think they represent a great story. Most importantly, they highlight the possibility of what technology could offer to businesses today. Not every business will exploit such advanced technologies, but they open up endless possibilities. Imagine being able to think of an idea and being able to validate it with your customers in a non-disruptive manner. If the idea has any legs, you are able to conduct stuff like A/B tests to quickly learn about it. Or, in the worst case, you drop the idea because there are no takers. Most importantly, you do that all in a matter of hours and days rather than weeks and months.

Welcome to the bold new world of continuous deployment, where the software you use is constantly being updated as it gets written. If a "release" was planned with some 50 features to be delivered in ten months and if the first few features are ready in the initial few months—enough to roll out a Minimum Viable Product (MVP)—then why not do a dark launch, some kind of private beta, or a by-invitation roll-out so that valuable feedback can be taken from the innovators or early adopters? As more features become ready, they keep getting pushed into production. Whenever users log into the service, they get the latest features that are in the production. Their usage pattern and feedback can help developers understand how users like the newly rolled out features. Developers can also learn about any major blind spots in terms of the user experience.

Why would someone do it? Well, imagine that being able to respond to customer behavior in real time could ensure higher engagement and monetization. For example, pretend you are selling vacation packages online, and there is a program on a popular lifestyle channel about a great vacation destination. You suddenly start seeing higher traffic from viewers who want to check out the destination. At that point, you might have a golden opportunity to respond to such a surge in traffic by making it easier for visitors to your web site to find the information they are looking for. Hopefully, you can convert them into customers.

I see the CI/CD pipeline as an integral part of the deployment pipeline for any modern software development process. Even if the software is offered as a non-online (or an "on-prem," meaning it is hosted on servers that are housed on-premises inside an enterprise, perhaps due to security or some other concern), the development process doesn't have to stop benefiting from a system that offers such continuous feedback.

---

[5]Velocity 2011: Jon Jenkins, "Velocity Culture," https://youtu.be/dxk8b9rSK0o

DevOps

When the Agile Manifesto came out in 2001, it was normal to have silos—especially between development and testing—with clearly divided roles and responsibilities. The manifesto propounded an environment with a higher amount of shared responsibility among all the team members. In short, it introduced the idea that great development teams were not just separated around functional specializations, but were built around them: "Developers who test, and Testers who develop."

Back in 2001, enterprise software was still an 800-pound gorilla. Getting developers and testers together was a big deal. Web-based software was just beginning to appear, and the then-recent success of the web was quickly vaporized with the dot-com meltdown. As a result, there were no compelling use cases when it came to online businesses that needed hosted software as a key resource. However, over time, we have seen more and businesses, from all walks of life, embrace the online world and have increasingly higher business happenings online.

DevOps takes this inclusive, holistic thinking to a new level. I like what John Allspaw talked about in his deck "10+ Deploys Per Day: Dev and Ops Cooperation at Flickr."[6]

"Ops who think like devs and Devs who think like ops"

So, what is this DevOps? Is it a process, a tool, a technique, a framework, or something else? I think it is more like a mindset—just like it all started as an agile mindset and an agile culture, DevOps is all about creating a culture in organizations that promotes a holistic product thinking without compartmentalizing the responsibilities. It promotes shared ownership of a product without apportioning the responsibilities between development and operations—one seeks to maximize disruption and rollout innovation while the other thrives on steady state to ensure uptime and usage experience. In DevOps world, the entire team must accept shared responsibility for both these important business activities. This is extremely important for any kind of product that offers online services.

However, this is still a new area, and we are sure to see more innovation in this space. Again, I believe this is an integral part of the agile product culture that promotes thinking about all the aspects of a product, including ops, rather than thinking of it as an afterthought. Most importantly, it seeks to remove the barrier between "us" vs. "them," whichever side of the product development equation you see yourself in.

---

[6]www.slideshare.net/jallspaw/10-deploys-per-day-dev-and-ops-cooperation-at-flickr.

Conclusions

Software delivery has come a long way from the multi-year release cycles in the past when the users had to wait for shipment of the next version CDs. We have come to the point where a new idea might only be hours away from being put in the hands of end users. We now have the technology and tools to take such new ideas right from ideation through production and test them in byte-size deployments. As a result, we can really understand what customers want and respond in real time to their desires.

Two major trends are interesting: online software consumption and startups. Startups, and more specifically the lean startups, are constantly trying out newer and better ways of doing business. Concepts like MVP are becoming an integral part of product lingo, and supporting infrastructure, such as CI/CD and DevOps, is making it possible for entrepreneurs and startups to experiment with partial functionality before committing to a bigger and longer investment timeframe. In addition, with more and more software being consumed online, the whole incremental delivery is even more powerful because there are virtually no marginal costs associated with the digital distribution of software.

In this final chapter, we have briefly looked at the ideas behind software delivery. My aim was to stitch up the entire value creation chain in the context of agile product development. While the aspect of software delivery is an important one, I consider it a necessary but not sufficient part of the product development. Once the deployment pipeline is set up (and if you have the right talent, it might require a few hours or a couple of days), it is available as the raw capability. With better technology and tools, it can be made extremely fast and efficient.

Version control, build and release infrastructure alone can't win you matches—for that, you still need rock-solid talent, However, you do need infrastructure to support and reinforce some of your process tasks that can be automated to the extent their execution is not only made lightning fast to eventually "run anytime, anywhere", even the human errors in delivery can be totally eliminated.

I realize that I might be oversimplifying the reality by saying it, but I do believe that infrastructure is (or it eventually must be) table stakes—if it continues to be "visible" to you daily, there is something wrong in the way you have implemented it. It should be the silent hum of the engine running somewhere in the background that ensures your teams can peacefully do why you hired them for in the first place—design innovative products that create customer value!

Welcome to the journey…

Index

Get the eBook for only $5!

Why limit yourself?

Now you can take the weightless companion with you wherever you go and access your content on your PC, phone, tablet, or reader.

Since you've purchased this print book, we're happy to offer you the eBook in all 3 formats for just $5.

Convenient and fully searchable, the PDF version enables you to easily find and copy code—or perform examples by quickly toggling between instructions and applications. The MOBI format is ideal for your Kindle, while the ePUB can be utilized on a variety of mobile devices.

To learn more, go to www.apress.com/companion or contact support@apress.com.

Printed in the United States
By Bookmasters